The Unholy War

Marius Baar

The
Unholy War

Thomas Nelson Publishers
Nashville

Contents

Dedication
and Acknowledgements

To all who suffer for their witness to Jesus Christ, to my dear wife, with whom I stood for many years on the front lines in the battle for the gospel, and to our many friends, this book is dedicated.

My appreciation goes to all my Swiss, German, and French friends who have made possible the appearance of this book through their contributions; to those who gave of their time and their knowledge as writers or translators; to the proofreaders; to those who encouraged me to write and helped me develop many of my ideas; and finally to all those who allowed me to quote from their articles without cost.

Marius Baar

Prefaces

Since the Yom Kippur War, who is not aware of the oil problem? For many people, the importance of this acute problem lies in the difficulty of obtaining energy supplies, disruption of economic equilibrium, reapportionment of the world's wealth, a decline of the Western powers, and other factors of the same order. Very few people perceive, behind the political and economic questions, the spectacular signs of a coming—or already present—Islamic rebirth. However understandable it may be that non-Christians see only the political and economic aspects of this historic event (as significant as the rebirth of Israel), it is paradoxical that Christians remain blind to a vital aspect of the situation. They fail to see that Islamic expansion, the rise of oil wealth, is aimed at spiritual conquest of the West.

It is to Marius Baar's credit that he draws our attention to these facts. He feels as responsible for his message as the apostle Paul: "Woe is me if I do not preach the gospel!" The Old Testament is full of examples of men who received a message from the Lord and spoke out; just so did the author see the necessity of writing this book. He is also particularly well-qualified to write it. His long career as a missionary, his knowledge of Arabic and of Islam, his thought and outlook—all these make him an expert in the field. We thank him for having shared his conclusions with us.

What he has to say is both convincing and compelling. It disturbs our preconceived notions and upsets our traditional ideas about the place of prophecy in our lives. Should the Christian view history through eyes conditioned by ancient prophecies? This is disturbing in an era of tolerance and "mutual respect." We would willingly sacrifice all notion of a divine plan to avoid the appearance of crusaders waging a holy war.

But it is thus that the prophecy will be fulfilled—in a political and economic context, in human history. It will pass from the timeless plane of sacred Scripture and become history, before we know it, before we hear the cry of alarm.

—M. Weyland M.D.
May 5, 1979

This is a fascinating book. A wealth of views, ideas, reflections, and inferences on economics, politics, and in particular, religion and eschatology make it absorbing reading.

When I first read the manuscript, I remembered the conversations I was privileged to have with the author in the early stages of is composition. I recall the impact his basic idea had upon me, as it emerged from the general line of his argument. This idea I would summarize in the following fashion: Two parallel lines of descent stem from Abraham. One line is that of his "natural" son Ishmael, born of the maidservant Hagar; he is the ancestor of the Arabs. Abraham's other son, Isaac, the son "of the promise" born of Sarah his wife, is the ancestor of the Jews. Jesus, the Christ promised from the beginning of the Old Testament, is Isaac's descendant. Isaac's line brought salvation into the world, though its final accomplishment is yet to come. This is the lineage of God, the Christian line. Ishmael's descendants include the Amalekites, the Philistines (all hereditary enemies of the Jews) and Mohammed, the founder of Islam. This is the anti-Christian line, and the two sets of descendants have always fought.

The author's historic and biblical vision gives rise to an astonishing conclusion: The political, economic, and religious system of the last days, represented in the Bible by the term "Antichrist," is to be found in Islam. Numerous citations from both the Bible and the Koran corrobate this view. It is not, however, an entirely new idea. In 1940, G. H. Lang wrote in *The Histories and Prophecies of Daniel* (Paternoster Press: 1940): "When Antichrist makes Babylon the center of world government, then his empire will become that depicted in all its realistic detail by the prophets of the Bible . . . Babylon is Satan's first and last center on earth, as Jerusalem is God's. And the center of gravity in the modern world is shifting continuously toward the Near East" (pages 189–90).

The large number of citations from diverse authors is

11

witness to the exhaustive research embodied in the present work. It is to be hoped that the reader will gain valuable new perspectives from reading it, and that, above all, he will heed the warning given in this pertinent work.

—Professor J. P. Schneider

Publisher's Foreword

The Unholy War was written by a man who takes the Bible seriously. He believes that God chose Abraham to be the father of a nation of people to whom He would give His love and care. And he believes that the nation of Israel, which is made up of descendants of Abraham, is the one God has chosen to be the center of world happenings.

But the author traces many of the current problems in the world right back to Abraham, for Abraham had two sons: The first was Ishmael who was born to the Egyptian maid Hagar; the second was Isaac who was born to Abraham's wife Sarah. Ishmael was Abraham's son "born according to the flesh," as the apostle Paul says in Galatians 4:29, because Abraham and Sarah did not believe that God would be able to give them their promised son. Paul calls Isaac the son "born according to the Spirit" and a child "of promise." God wanted to carry on Abraham's line through Isaac and thereby establish the people of Israel from whom would come the Messiah, the Savior of the world.

Ishmael and Isaac never got along. Although Hagar and her son were rejected, Abraham prayed for God's

13

blessing on both sons. The struggle between the two has never ended, and in these last days of world history it has developed into a deadly hatred.

The Jewish people and the modern state of Israel are descendants and heirs of Abraham. They are children of promise, and God will keep His promises. Ishmael became the father of the Arabs. They are being united today religiously by Islam and economically by the industrial power of oil. This book shows clearly that throughout history there has been a struggle between the God of Israel, Jehovah, and His opponent, who is represented by Allah, the god of Islam.

The West now stands at a crossroads. Whose side will it be on? Ishmael's or Isaac's? Allah's or Jehovah's? This book should not be read casually. The author carefully fits one piece after another into the Middle East puzzle until the reader can see a powerful and shocking picture of how the events of today fit into the predictions of the Bible.

It is our prayer that many readers will thoroughly study the material presented in this book and will come to terms with it. Until now, the prophetic views discussed here have been seen from a different angle and biblical statements have been interpreted in other ways. But considering the weight of proof offered by current events, it is easy to agree with the author's arguments.

Introduction

"Hail to the prophet!" shouted thousands of people as the Ayatollah Khomeini took control of Iran in the name of Allah. What has happened in Iran is a signal for the world and especially for Christians, for it is one more sign of the end times as predicted in Scripture. Have we understood its significance or will we ignore this warning, as we did in the oil crisis of 1973?

Islam, the power that had long been thought to be dead, has come to life again. Islamic countries are preparing to return to the pure doctrine of the prophet Mohammed and enforce the legal and moral teachings of the Koran again. The Koran is said to be Allah's last revelation and is to be obeyed not only by Muslims (Moslems) but by all mankind. It is Allah's will that all men be united under the Islamic banner at the end of the world.

In the last few years, one man believing "*Allah hu akbar*" ("Allah is the most high God") has succeeded in shaking the Middle East and the whole world. The triumph of the Ayatollah Khomeini is not just over the dynasty of the Shah of Iran, but over all world powers. Just as Gamal Abdel Nasser showed Western Europe and the world that Europe's power had been broken by Arab nationalism, so the Ayatollah Khomeini has demonstrated to the world that a militant Islam can bring America and the West to their knees. In a very short time the center of world events has been moved to the Middle East. Biblical prophecy has become modern history, and we are eyewitnesses to it!

> The LORD your God will raise up for you a prophet like me from among you, from your countrymen, you shall listen to him (Deut. 18:15).

Islam claims that Mohammed is the prophet promised by God in Deuteronomy 18:15. It also teaches that in the end times a prophet will appear who will subdue the world. The Islamic leaders are therefore convinced that their hour has come. Islam is becoming a world power. We are witnessing the unification of the Islamic world, supported by the economic might of oil. The world has rejected the prophets that came from the line of Abraham, Isaac, and Jacob. Will it now follow the prophet from the line of Abraham and Ishmael? Moslems are convinced that Allah ". . . hath sent his apostle [Mohammed] with guidance and the religion of truth, that, though they hate it who join other gods with God, He may make it victorious over every other religion" (sura 61:9).

Whether the world follows Jesus or Mohammed, God has said, "Surely the LORD God does nothing/ Unless he reveals His secret counsel to His servants the prophets" (Amos 3:7). The God whose name is Jehovah in the Old Testament and who sent His Son Jesus Christ in the New Testament has ordained the events now taking place and those that will take place.

I do not intend to accuse anyone in this book. Rather, I will simply state facts, express my amazement, and confess that everything seems to be unfolding according to the biblical plan. However, those who do not fully acknowledge the truth of the Bible will not grasp the deeper significance of current events. The more seriously we take the Bible, the clearer we will understand the message of this book. Only our omniscient God is able to reveal the future to us.

> All the nations have gathered together
> In order that the peoples may be assembled.
> Who among them can declare this
> And proclaim to us the former things?
> Let them present their witnesses that they may
> be justified,
> Or let them hear and say, "It is true" (Is. 43:9).

I do not claim to have the only correct prophetic view of what is happening. However, due to my experience of many years with Islam and with the gospel, I have gained an understanding of this awakening Middle Eastern giant. Thus I believe that I have a message for our times, even if it does not fit well into many peoples' worldview. If it comes as a shock to some, may it be a beneficial one!

I have lived among Moslems for about twenty-five years, and I count many of them as my friends. Among them is the sultan of the area where I worked as a missionary. He owes his life to my wife's nursing care. I also know some Moslem priests (*fakis*).

Assembling this book has taken many years of gathering piece after piece. It was only after studying

INTRODUCTION

the Koran, Islam, and the Arabs that I realized there are only two choices left for us today: The chaos of a world turning more and more away from God, or the true church of Jesus Christ whose redemption is drawing near (see Luke 21:28).

No man knows the day or the hour of the end of the age, but certain signs have been given to us. If we do not listen to the prophetic passages of Scripture and are surprised by the Lord's return, we will be without excuse. God has spoken through both the Old and New Testaments; the Bible is the only revelation of God, inspired by the Holy Spirit. Listen to what it has to say about the time in which we live!

The Unholy War

The caption on this Iranian placard reads: " 'The final victory will come when our entire nation has accepted Islam. But beyond that, another victory must be won: The international triumph of Islam and the building of its kingdom over the whole world,' said the Ayatollah Khomeini."

1

The World in Crisis

The West is at a crossroads.

The future of Western civilization as we know it will be determined, I believe, by which direction we go in taking sides with either Israel or the Arab countries. In years past, we could be neutral, maintaining good relations with both sides in their numerous struggles with each other. But the Arabs now have us over a barrel—an oil barrel—and will not allow the West the luxury of remaining neutral. A short course in history explains why.

Isaac and Ishmael in the Past

Amazingly, the roots of this current world crisis are found some four thousand years ago in Mesopotamia (today's Iraq), home of a man named Abraham. He lived among a people who worshiped many gods. On one particular day the one true God, Jehovah, the Father of our Lord Jesus Christ, revealed Himself to Abraham and told him to leave his homeland (although He did not tell Abraham where he was going). God also promised Abraham, who was married but childless, that he would have a great number of descendants.

As time went on Abraham's faith was severely tested because it seemed that God would not keep His promise. Sarah, Abraham's wife, had grown well past the age of being able to conceive, and yet she still had no children. And so Sarah begged Abraham to have a child by her Egyptian maid Hagar. Acting in disobedience, trying to fulfill the promises of God Himself rather than letting God do so, Abraham had a son, Ishmael, by Hagar.

Fourteen years later the promised son, Isaac, was born to Abraham and his wife Sarah, and each son became the forefather of twelve tribes: Ishmael the father of the Arabs, Isaac the father of the Jews. Abraham foresaw the animosity that would develop between the two half-brothers—animosity which has continued until today—and asked God to bless Ishmael even before Isaac's birth. God granted this request as follows:

> And Abraham said to God, "Oh that Ishmael might live before Thee!" But God said, "No, but Sarah your wife shall bear you a son, and you shall call his name Isaac; and I will establish My covenant with him for an everlasting covenant for his descendants after him. And as for Ishmael, I have heard you; behold, I will bless him, and will make him fruitful, and will multiply him exceedingly. He shall become the father of twelve princes, and I will make him a great nation. But My covenant I will establish with Isaac, whom Sarah will bear to you at this season next year" (Gen. 17:18-21).

Ishmael (the Arabs) has never gotten over the fact

that Isaac (the Jews) is God's chosen one and the bearer of God's promises. This helps explain why the Koran claims that Arabs are special in Allah's (god's) eyes and explains the struggles we see today over the land of Israel. Throughout history, Isaac and his descendants have represented the fulfillment of the promises of God while Ishmael and his descendants have represented the efforts of man to do things on his own (see Gal. 4:22–30).

Isaac and Ishmael in the Future

Christians have always been convinced that Israel would play a key role in the end times. But seldom has anyone dealt with the question of the role Ishmael would play. God prepared Christ's first coming through the people of Israel; today He is preparing Christ's second coming through the same people. But at the same time Satan is preparing the revealing of a godless one. The Bible says that when Israel has completely returned to its homeland, the Beast and the False Prophet will appear.

> And the beast was taken, and with him the false prophet who worked signs in his presence, by which he deceived those who had received the mark of the beast and those who worshiped his image. These two were cast alive into the lake of fire burning with brimstone (Rev. 19:20).

Second Thessalonians 2:3 speaks as well of the "man of sin."

> Let no one deceive you by any means; for that

23

> Day will not come unless the falling away comes first, and the man of sin is revealed, the son of perdition.

Nineteen hundred years ago the apostle John said that the spirit of antichrist was *already* in the world (see 1 John 4:3). Just as the Jewish people are being prepared for the second coming of Christ, other people are being prepared for the coming of the False Prophet.

Two forces are confronting each other: God and Satan—Good and Evil—Light and Darkness—Truth and Falsehood—Life and Death. God and Satan have always battled for the souls of men. But that battle is about to come to a dramatic culmination. There is no neutral ground. Whoever is not on God's side is on the side of Satan.

It is important, then, that we be attentive to what is happening in the Middle East, the place where the last act of the human drama will be played.

From a historical perspective, almost overnight the center of world events has switched to the Middle East. The Islamic countries are becoming more and more powerful, forcing a confrontation with Israel. However, history shows that wherever Arabs have lived they have left desolation behind. I observed this personally during my years in Africa. And the West is already becoming a desert through the "blessing" of oil which has polluted our environment. Moreover, if the countries of the Middle East shut off oil they are now selling to us, it will mean the fall of the West.

But even beyond that, the spiritual desolation that will come in the end times will be worse than any physical desolation. And the signs of that spiritual desolation are already at hand. "He who has an ear, let him hear what the Spirit says to the churches . . ." (Rev. 2:7), and "Blessed is he who reads . . . the words of this prophecy . . ." (Rev. 1:3).

I know that my interpretation of current events will be rejected by many people. My desire is to give you a specific world view of the coming times. Only at the end of the present age will the glory of Jesus Christ be revealed. And the only accurate guide through these times is the Bible, God's inspired Word revealed to us by His Spirit. Let me challenge you with the words of the apostle John.

> Beloved, do not believe every spirit, but test the spirits whether they are of God; because many false prophets have gone out into the world. By this you know the spirit of God: Every spirit that confesses that Jesus Christ has come in the flesh is of God, and every spirit that does not confess that Jesus Christ has come in the flesh is not of God. And this is the spirit of the Antichrist, which you have heard was coming, and even now it is already in the world. You are of God, little children, and have overcome them, because He who is in you is greater than he who is in the world. They are of the world. Therefore they speak as of the world, and the world hears them. We are of God. He who knows God hears us; he who is not of God does not hear us. By this we know the spirit of truth and the spirit of error (1 John 4:1–6).

The spirit that denies that Jesus Christ is the Son of

God who came in the flesh has, from the beginning, tried again and again to destroy God's plan for Israel and the church. And this spirit is at work today.

The Decline of the West

The years after World War II have been years of defeat for the West. The Western powers have come to be viewed as weaklings, growing daily more impotent in the eyes of the Third World. Aleksandr Solzhenitsyn has said,

> The Western powers, who were all-powerful in 1945, have freely given up, under the influence of public opinion, position after position and country after country without one shot being fired. The victorious powers have become the conquered ones.

This decline has come about because of a loss of spiritual goals. Christ commanded His church to evangelize the world. But the church in the West has lost sight of evangelization and concentrated instead on Christianization and imperialism. We have failed and forfeited our rights as the leading force in the world. It is now time for another power to assume leadership in the world. Abdullah writes,

> Tell all men that the end is near for Christianity; the triumph of Islam is at hand. Show mankind the way to true Islam; give Christians the opportunity to know themselves and be converted.[1]

Arabs and Europeans

From their very beginning, followers of Mohammed sought to dominate other countries and conquer Europe, not by conversion but by force. In the sixth and seventh centuries the followers of Islam swept out of Arabia to claim the Holy Land and what is now the region of Turkey. They then spread westward across northern Africa, conquering the fertile Nile Valley and seizing control of Africa's lucrative slave trade. They forced the Coptic church to accept Islam and all but

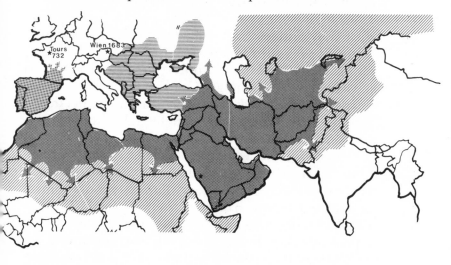

Islamic expansion to the eighth century A.D.
Conquests of the Ottoman Empire from the thirteenth to the seventeenth centuries.
Islamic expansion in Africa and Asia to the seventeenth century.
Reconquered territories by the Christians from the eighth to the seventeenth centuries.

27

destroyed the influence of Christianity on the African continent.

In 711, the Moors (a militant clan of African Muslims) crossed the Strait of Gibraltar and took Spain. They pressed across the Pyrenees Mountains and would have taken France as well, had they not been turned back by Charles Martel's army at the Battle of Tours in 732. The Moors fell back to make Spain their stronghold, establishing an Islamic capital at Cordova.

Though Christian nations waged the Crusades against the Turkish Muslims in Palestine from 1096 to 1270, they were unable to dislodge the Turks from their holy shrines. Not until 1492 were the Roman Catholic rulers Ferdinand and Isabella able to take Granada, the last Moorish fortress in Spain. The Muslims held a tenacious grip on the lands they conquered. Even when they were defeated militarily, they continued to influence the thought and culture of the Christian West.

In 1683, Vienna, which was considered the stronghold of Christianity, was besieged by Islamic Turks. Weakened by religious wars, Europe almost came under the domination of Islam. At that time the Christian West nearly ceased to exist. One history text reports, " 'The Christian faith is a hairsbreadth from its downfall if you are victorious here,' said Tekeli to the Turkish Vezir who nearly succeeded in making Europe Islamic in 1683."[2] But the West united and drove the Turks from Europe.

Perhaps God allowed Europe to dominate the world since the Reformation so that His Word might be preached throughout the world.

Just as Israel rejected Christ and was scattered throughout the world, so the West has resisted God's Word and is experiencing its political downfall. Before its final dispersion, Israel was given the choice of Christ or Barabbas. We today are given the choice of Christ or Mohammed. What the followers of Mohammed could not accomplish for more than one thousand years with force, they are now accomplishing with cunning: the domination of the West.

The key, of course, is oil.

Life without oil is unthinkable, and oil is being used as a means of coercion. For instance, in November, 1973, most European nations voted for a United Nations (UN) resolution against Israel. With that resolution much of the world made a definite move toward the Islamic camp. In November, 1975, Zionism was condemned by the UN, the first step in what might lead to Israel's exclusion from the world body.

But in the end it is not just a question of Israel, but of truth versus error. If we reject Israel, we reject its history and with it the foundation of the New Testament. We are chopping down the tree into which we as Christians are grafted (see Rom. 11).

Islam Against the Peacock Throne

One of the West's strongest allies in the Middle East was Iran. Although the nation was ninety-three percent Moslem, the late Shah, the "Light of the Aryans," nonetheless developed a strong country that was friendly to the West. Who would have thought that he could have lost his power so quickly? Or who would

29

have thought that Islam would attempt to stem such progress in order to reintroduce Islamic laws and chronology?

Since the mullahs have taken power, violent changes have taken place in Iran. Israel used to get its oil from Iran. Now this country is taking a hard line advocating the destruction of Israel. Europe is coming under increasing pressure to take a stand against Israel through an Arab oil boycott against nations friendly to Israel.

The late Shah was quoted as saying, "If this part of the world goes to ruin, it will drag Europe with it. I'm afraid that's going to happen."[3] While we live as though things are continuing normally, the world situation is changing daily and Islam is becoming more powerful. In Iran, Islam has succeeded in toppling one of the mightiest dynasties in the world. This should be an alarm to the West. With the Shah's deposal and passing, an important factor in slowing the spread of Islam and the expansion of its empire has been removed. The development of the Arab-Islamic bloc will no longer be hindered, but I believe will even be encouraged and supported by Western powers. The way is being paved for the final confrontation with Israel.

Yasir Arafat, head of the Palestinian Liberation Organization (PLO), knew that the explosive power of Islam was greater than the power of weapons of war. In 1978 he went on a pilgrimage to Mecca to renew his alliance with Allah. What nationalism, terrorism, and war cannot bring about will be accomplished in the name of Allah—and with the power of oil. In his name, millions of Moslems can be mobilized and united in a common purpose. In the name of Allah, the Middle East will rise up united against the West and force it to its knees. I predict all the world leaders will stand behind the Islamic union and will remain silent when the destruction of Israel is undertaken. In the future, the economy and the survival of any nation will depend on its disposition toward Israel.

These signs confirm to me that we are living in the final stages of world history. We are lacking only that one man who will seek to lead the world out of its economic crisis in return for giving him honor. Tomorrow he could rise up like an Ayatollah Khomeini and unhinge the whole Middle East, and with it the world. No longer is the question *whether* he will arise, but only *when* will he come to power.

The West is taking one blow after another without learning its lesson. Perhaps it is now too late, as events seem to be out of control. People are being executed daily in Iran. Just before each execution, the executioner yells, *"Bismellahi!"* ("In the name of Allah!"). *Khomeini even executed the general who had saved his life by pleading for him to the Shah!* The elite are being eliminated, and the nation is being catapulted back into the Middle Ages.

One should be able to see from all this how merciless Islam is. Anything that gets in the way is simply destroyed. The future may hold such destruction for us. All it will take is a transition from control by oil to control by religion. We have *already fallen* into the economic trap. We could also fall into a spiritual trap. Oil has brought world power to Islam, and by means of it the followers of Mohammed are seeking to bring about a global religion.

Lebanon and Malta

Two other parts of the world where the Moslems are demonstrating their plan for world domination are Lebanon and Malta. Lebanon is the only Middle Eastern country in which Christians have constitutional rights to participate in the government. Such cooperation is a thorn in the side of Moslems in the same way the state of Israel or a future Palestinian state with "equal rights for Jews and Moslems" is an impossibility from the Islamic perspective.

According to a 1975 brochure, *The Middle East at the Crossroads* by Konrad Meyer, the Lebanese civil war is a religious problem. The Muslims want this "foreign body" removed from the eye of the Middle East.

A newspaper article in 1978 explained that the West is impotent because of economic pressure.

> The world's conscience is still tormented by the thoughts of the terrible suffering of the Jewish people. Thus we cannot stand by and do nothing about the tragic fate of two million Lebanese Christians. We live in an absurd era in which government morality is subject to economic considerations and sins of omission are committed daily. Can the West permit a people to be eliminated and an independent state to be sacrificed to economic interests which depend only on Arab oil? Let there be no mistake: the program of the Islamic block includes not only the subjugation of the Middle East, but the whole world.[4]

But Lebanon is not an isolated example of the Moslem intent to subjugate the world. This can also be seen in Turkey, in Chad, in Iran, and in Malta.

In March, 1979, the British took down the Union Jack for the last time on the island of Malta in the Mediterranean. For 180 years the British had controlled the path to the Suez from "the unsinkable aircraft carrier," as Churchill once called the island. The British left and the Arabs came. Colonel Mummar el-Qaddafi of Libya arrived at the farewell festivities with sultans on bejeweled horses and eight hundred Libyans distributing the "green Bible" of Qaddafi. Libya now wants to pour money into Malta and dictator Qaddafi will lay out money only in the name of Allah.

Has Islam made its first European conquest in Malta?

From Camels to Jets

While the economies of the West suffer from inflation and unfavorable balances of payment due to the increasing cost of oil from the Middle East, a new Golden Age is dawning on the Persian Gulf. The Arab economic miracle has begun.

There has not been a comparable accumulation of wealth in the Middle East since the days of Solomon. He possessed a mere fourteen hundred chariots; the sheiks possess cars, planes, and palaces. Solomon had his horses brought to him in caravans from Egypt; the sheiks have their limousines flown to them from Europe or America. Anton Zischka writes:

The shining symbol of the new Riyadh (the

33

From camel to limousine. In Abu Dhabi the per capita income is very high, and every citizen receives a rent-free apartment. Electric, telephone, and water bills are unknown. This is no fairy tale but stark reality.

Saudi Arabian capital) is the Nadjaridje Palace, which the king has floodlit at night like a cathedral. It has the world's largest air-conditioning system, its own zoo, and a garage for more than a thousand cars. Within its walls are four palaces for the king's four wives and the royal court, 37 villas for the princes and 32 villas for concubines.

There are also schools, a hospital, and a museum. The construction costs of this palace-city, in which 6,000 people reside and which can hold 20,000 guests, are said to have been around $350 million. [5]

What seems like a tale from *The Arabian Nights* is today a stark reality. In Abu Dhabi, the largest sheikdom in the federation of United Arab Emirates located on the Persian Gulf, citizens enjoy one of the world's highest per capita incomes. Free homes, electricity, and water are provided. Telephone calls around the world can be made free through the government-owned satellite. Citizens of Abu Dhabi—and other sheikdoms—can do their business with any stock exchange or bank on earth in a few minutes. There are no taxes. There is no duty on imported goods. The citizens consider themselves, in a way, members of the ruler's family.

If a citizen of Abu Dhabi becomes ill, he receives treatment in an ultramodern hospital. If his case is too complicated to be treated there, he is flown, free of cost, to a foreign country, often with an accompanying relative. As if from Aladdin's lamp, millions of dollars flow daily into the benevolent ruler's coffers.

Much of the work force in Abu Dhabi—and other

Arab lands—is made up of foreigners: Africans, Pakistanis, Indians, Japanese, Germans, and Americans. The hotels are booked up constantly—for months, even years ahead—because businessmen from industrial countries are forced to wait days or weeks to get an audience with the sheik. And without his blessing, their factories and businesses would be sure failures.

Not long ago it was a rarity to see a light on the desert. Now the desert glows with lights. Not long ago camel caravans moved from oasis to oasis with their few goods at thirty miles per day. Today, Land Rovers and fully air-conditioned limousines travel over asphalt roads and even a few four-lane highways.

The amount of money the sheiks have is incomprehensible to most of us. There is so much "black gold" in the ground that they have no idea how they will dispose of this "blessing" of Allah.

A hotel manager from the Black Forest told me recently that a man from an emirate stopped at his hotel. His outward appearance was so disheveled that the manager wondered if he could pay. When the manager asked for payment, the man reached in his pocket and laid $18,000 on the desk, asking if that would cover his bill.

Another guest from an oil country saw some artificial flowers in a window of a hotel. He ordered $15,000 worth of them for his palace and paid a first-class airline ticket so the manager could arrange them herself in his palace.

In July, 1980, thieves broke into a Riviera home and stole $150,000 in currency from a bedside table and $20 million in jewelry. The only way the owner, a sheik who reputedly gambled $350,000 a night in local casinos, knew the value of the jewelry was by appraising similar collections he had given to each of his three other wives.

On the Riviera, seventy percent of the luxury villas have changed owners. British and American people of means are selling out to the Arabs. A trip to the Riviera is simply a short hop in a private jet for a sheik.

Whereas in Europe and America it has taken years of discipline and hard work to arrive at our current state of technology, it has taken the Arabs only a few years and much less work to far surpass our standard of living. The know-how comes from Europe, America, and Japan. The work force comes from the Third World. Affluence is being served to the Arabs on a silver platter. Is it any wonder they are filled with thanksgiving to Allah and are motivated to spread Islam throughout the world?

Oil, Islam, and the Industrial Nations

It is important for us to know how the Arabs will use their riches and their power, for that will obviously determine the course of history in the short-term. The danger lies, again, in their conviction that Allah has blessed them in these end times so that the world may come under Islamic domination.

Financial analysts estimate that Middle East oil nations may amass more than $500 billion of investment money in the next five years. This sum would have brought *every* share traded on the New York Stock Exchange in 1978 and 1979![6]

It should not be surprising, then, that American banks are turning away from Israel and becoming more and more bound to the "Arab lobby." Business and industry are already trembling before this rising Middle East giant, afraid of getting on its "boycott list." Their threat is real for, as Zaki Yamani said, "Our weapon—oil—is much more powerful than you might think. We can cut back production eight per cent with no effect. If need be, we can stop exports for months without suffering. But how could you survive that?"

Moreover, the Moslems are willing to sacrifice for Allah. In a speech made in Damascus in June, 1979, Colonel Qaddafi said he would not consider it a sacrifice to return to his parents' roots in the desert and live on dates and camel's milk.

But is the West willing to sacrifice? During the oil embargo of 1973-74, I read in a Swiss newspaper, "longing for freedom and serenity, mankind will never sell its soul for oil. We Swiss will refuse to bow to the turban."

I wish the author were right. But the sad truth is that the Arabs could bring Europe—including Switzerland—to the point of starvation in only three years. Without the approval of the Arabs, we will neither buy nor sell. And no nation can survive the collapse of its economy. The Arabs are certainly not bothered by the increasing debts of the Americans and Europeans; it simply means they will be increasingly dependent on them. The Arabs don't need our money; we do need their oil (and their money).

Thus, the events of the 1973-74 oil embargo effectively brought us into the Arab camp. Since that time, the Arabs to an increasing extent have controlled the economic and financial affairs of the world through their oil. The Middle East is a conglomerate of economic, military, political, and religious forces such as the world has never experienced. *Time* magazine reported,

> The consequences of the battle for oil extend far beyond the Israeli-Arab dispute. Since the second World War, no single issue has appeared with such implications or caused such worldwide turmoil. Even if the Arabs should open up the oil tap to everyone tomorrow, the world would no longer be the same.

An encyclopedia article agreed:

> In any case, one thing is certain: The history of the last quarter of the twentieth century will not be written without the Arabs. [7]

And a French scientist described the awakening of Islam as follows:

> Islam was in a long sleep, near death. Most of what happened in the world happened without it. It had lost everything. But its sleep did not last long enough to obliterate its past accomplishments. Its culture, its art treasures, and its moral force, however, were covered with dust. The sleeper is now awakening. The Moslem's eyes are now wide open, and his mind is clear. He has re-opened his Koran, and a program of action is in his head. A powerful program!
>
> The Mohammedan remains inwardly totally Moslem, even when he no longer firmly holds to

39

his faith. He differs in this from many Christians, who are only nominally Christian or go to church out of tradition only. The Moslem's religion forms his whole existence. Come what may, he will remain a Moslem.[8]

The awakening of the Arab giant will mean not just the awakening of a group of people, but world domination by them. For four hundred years the Arabs awaited their *baath* (resurrection), and now the brute is stirring! No statesman in the world could have foreseen such an overnight change in fortune. But today, 130 million Arabs long for the renewed unity and greatness of an Islamic Empire stretching from Morocco to the Persian Gulf. To such an empire could be added as close allies the other 470 million Moslems of the world.

Islamic power already is astounding, and it will grow greater. In Paris the Arabs own the "Tour Manhattan." In Strasbourg, Saudi Arabia is financing construction of a huge business and apartment complex. In Germany, Kuwait bought 14.6 percent of Daimler-Benz, the car manufacturer.

With their billions, the Arabs can shake any currency system in the world to its foundations. Most Western countries are experiencing balance of trade deficits, due primarily to oil purchases. Iran has lent money to the World Bank, the total loan now standing at $350 billion.

Sheik Saba al-Salim Al Sabah, the Emir of Kuwait, bought the American island of Kawa for the sum of $17.4 million. On this island, off the coast of South Carolina, he will construct a $100 million super-luxury tourist center. He will also make his own residence there, costing around $50 million. Oil concessions bring in $180 million per week to the emirate.[9]

In 1977 and 1978, the First Arabian Corporation bought four first-class hotels in Paris: The Grand Hotel, the Prince of Wales, the Meurice, and the Cafe de Paris. At the beginning of 1979 it bought the Ritz-Paris-Holding. In this dream hotel, the construction and outfitting of a single room would cost $100,000 today. It is estimated that the First Arabian Corporation paid $25 million for the hotel, but this astronomical figure represents but five percent of the Arabs' daily oil production.

Oil: A Gift from Allah?

At one time conflicts in the Far East, Africa, and elsewhere left us undisturbed. Those places were far away. They caused us little inconvenience. At the most we felt some sympathy for those we saw in magazines or on television who were involved in struggles. But the turn of events in the Middle East will affect us all. If oil stops, so will our cars, trucks, tractors, and fishing boats. If oil stops, industry will come to a standstill. Enormous unemployment will ruin the framework of our society. Our homes will not be heated, and cars, planes, and tanks will become useless museum pieces.

Never before has civilized man been so dependent on a form of energy controlled to such an extent by one group of people. Before World War II it was possible to get by without Middle Eastern oil. But never again will that be the case. Any world power with such control over an important energy source would exploit the circumstances for its own gain. But the fact that the oil producers are motivated by a religious fervor makes the situation doubly serious.

It has been predicted that by 1985 there could be

The destiny of the world depends on the vital artery which provides oil from the Persian Gulf for the industrial countries.

42

$500 billion piled up in the Middle East for which there is no immediate use. Such wealth could buy up much of the European Common Market and maybe more. Dr. Saeb Jarudi, chairman of the Arabic Fund of Social and Economic Development, said, 'We will possess the two decisive economic factors: the capital and the energy reserves of the world.' "[10]

2

Arab Unity

The Moslems consider oil a gift from Allah for the purpose of making Islam a leading force in the world. Can it be merely coincidence that Ishmael and Isaac have both moved suddenly to the center stage of world events? The Bible speaks clearly of the restoration of Israel and also of an ungodly system that will try to exterminate Israel.

"The Arab states are waiting for a man who will unite them in a Greater Arab Empire," said a Palestinian to me in 1977. The powers this man will possess will be political, economic, and military, but above all religious. The coming battle in the Middle East, into which the whole world will be drawn, will become a religious battle—an unholy war.

The unity of Arabs has been an important goal for many years.

> The *Sunday Times* of London reports events which must seem totally absurd to a Western observer. One of their editors, on a visit to the Arab countries, came across a copy of a small brochure in Arabic. The title: "Economic interests in the service of the Arab cause." It was

stamped "Strictly Confidential." The content proved to be the most ingenious plan that the Arab governments had ever worked out. It contained documents of a pan-Arab strategy for crisis situations. Three leading Arab economists had worked out a concept in 230 pages which could change conditions for all the Arab nations in a few months.

This highly confidential manuscript, drawn up for presentation to the economic commission of the Arab League, contains more than just measures for the use of oil as a tool of foreign policy; it contains a plan for the future by which the most divergent forces among the 125 million people between Casablanca and Kuwait can be molded together. The *Sunday Times* calls it a "master plan."[1]

Gamal Abdel Nasser of Egypt succeeded in bringing a temporary and partial Arab unity. Qaddafi of Libya envisions a future Arab unity. "We are the doormat of the world, but we shall change that!" he has said. No language other than that of the Koran is allowed any more in Libya. No official will answer a question in anything but Arabic, even if he is able to.

Just recently, I visited Tripoli and found that even the signs pointing to the restrooms were written only in Arabic. Qaddafi has also influenced other countries to eliminate French and switch completely to Arabic. "All Arabs will be united under the banner of Islam," Qaddafi has said.

120 million Arabs are awaiting the new prophet;

they are hoping he will come soon and build the Greater Arab Empire out of eighteen Arab states. They want the world to look on the resurrected Kalif-Empire with respect.

The dreamt-of fatherland is rich. The welfare of the citizens is assured by the billions of dollars of income. Poverty and hunger will vanish and justice will reign. The new prophet will be socialist, but not Marxist. His belief in Allah must be unshakable.

Islam possesses the spiritual might to realize this dream. Its beliefs, instituted by Mohammed 1300 years ago, are more than the moral codex for order on earth and the assurance of a place in the hereafter—Islam is meant to be a political doc-trine, revolutionary and expansive. Once before, it attempted the conquest of Europe. It was stopped, however, in France and Vienna.

The Arab nationalists want to correct the course of history. The coming prophet will again unfurl the banner of Islam and attempt the conquest of Europe anew. Europe is supposed to pay for the fact that it had looked down on the "Oriental camel drivers." But as long as the prophet re-mains unrevealed, the dream will remain un-realized.[2]

The future empire will be *Al Uma el Arabia,* and only the naive can fail to see it coming. Biblical prophecy clearly reveals both the restoration of the nation of Israel and the rise of the Arab Empire, which will geographically surround Israel. Although everything seems now to be in a state of flux, Ishmael's basic nature has remained unchanged for millenia.

Three areas in which the Arabs have already demonstrated a strong sense of unity are their boycott of any organization or country cooperating with Israel, their desire for an atomic bomb, and their domination of world currency. Let us briefly look at all three.

Boycott

Economic pressure in the form of a boycott is being applied to any organization or country that does business with Israel. A boycott office in Damascus, Syria, registers firms and individuals whose business is not desired in the Arab world because of their cooperation with Israel. Since March, 1979, Iran has also participated in this boycott with its own boycott office in Tehran. This office is managed mainly by members of the PLO. Examples of the boycott abound.

> Five Arab nations protested to the Belgian government in February, 1976, that the world Jewish congress was being held there. The Brussels foreign ministry had to answer Saudi Arabia, Iraq, Syria, Algeria, and Egypt that they could not prohibit the congress because of their constitution, as long as the participants guaranteed peace and order in the proceedings. It was added that the government was providing the world Jewish congress neither protection nor any other support.[3]

> The Arabs and apparently many Black African states boycotted the Israeli representative at the

THE UNHOLY WAR

world trade conference in Nairobi by marching
out of the auditorium or by staying away al-
together.[4]

Many U.S. firms are boycotting Israel. Many
have met the Arab demands in the second half of
1975 to do just that. Half of the 637 firms checked
admitted to having given in to Arab demands
between January 1, 1974 and December 5, 1975.
They also said they had made total sales of 352
million dollars with the Arabs in this same
period.[5]

At the beginning of 1973, Niger, Mali, and Chad
broke off diplomatic relations with Israel under Arabic
pressure. Israeli ambassadors and staffs were given
twenty-four hours to leave. These nations had been
promised great sums of money to do this. On April 29,
1973, the Organization for African Unity unanimously
adopted a resolution calling for sanctions against Israel.

Countries that send oil to Israel have been boycot-
ted, *even if the oil does not originate in Arab countries.*
Thousands of firms are on the boycott list. A single
lucrative business deal with the Arabs can entice a firm
to stop doing business with Israel. Since in the world
of business and industry in the West the ultimate goals
are profits and accumulation of capital—even at the
expense of Christian principles, we can tell in ad-
vance what choice our corporations will make. There
is no neutrality in this battle for survival.

The Arab Atom Bomb

America and the remainder of the West are being

48

outwitted with more and more finesse. We have dug our own grave. Ironically we have helped our enemies become world powers through our own lust for profits and our own love of economic competition. We sell weapons to our enemies and thus quicken our own—and others'—downfall.

More and more countries are arming themselves, and no one yet seems to take disarmament seriously. The Islamic world wants to join the nuclear fraternity. It is generally known that Qaddafi is willing to pay any conceivable price for the production of an Arab atomic bomb. It may not be far away.

Pakistan has built one but has not yet detonated it. The material for the bomb came from European countries. Pakistan is an Islamic state and it, too, is eyeing Jerusalem. Its president, General Mohammed Zia ul-Haq, is likewise convinced that Islam has been ordained by Allah to rule the world. And the atom bomb can be an instrument in attaining that goal. The apostle John said that the Beast will perform great and miraculous signs, ". . . so that he makes fire come down from heaven on the earth in the sight of men" (Rev. 13:13). Could the bomb and this prophetic word be connected?

World Currency

For many years the American dollar has been the standard world currency. In 1977 America's balance of payments deficit was $14,068 million. In 1978 the total was $14,529 million. The deficit dropped to $788 million in 1979, but this was still a sobering total.[6] The currencies in European countries are no longer stable since they have little of real value to back them up. The gold standard—long the foundation of currencies—is no longer considered reliable. What good would gold do us anyway, if an oil boycott paralyzed our industry and agriculture?

The following newspaper report demonstrates the Arabs' intention to become the dominate force in world currency regulation.

> The Arabs continue to work toward a strengthening of their economies and currencies. For example, an Arabian-Kuwaiti commission proposed the creation of seventeen amalgamated companies between the two lands. They are exploring the possibilities of a Persian Gulf Common Market.

> The currency authorities of Bahrain, Qatar, the United Emirates, and the Sultanate of Oman intend to extend the current Arabian-Kuwaiti accords to include themselves. These accords could lead, according to European observers, to an Arab economic and currency union, which seems much easier to bring into being than was the Common Market; after all, all the governments involved have budget surpluses. This could only mean a further worsening of the state of the American dollar.[7]

If an Arabic currency were to become the standard against which other countries' currencies are measured, it would be the most stable currency in the world, backed by energy reserves indispensable at the current time to modern civilization.

OPEC has said it wants to relinquish the dollar as the leading currency, according to the Arab weekly *Arab Report and Memo*. Rumors as to the relinquishing of the dollar, no longer a novelty, were strengthened in mid-July when a conference was held in London about the consequences of the fall of the dollar. Observers noted that the Saudis, strongest supporters of the dollar, showed themselves to be much more compromising now.[8]

No Unity in the West

The West no longer has a unifying spiritual commitment. In Europe, the Word of God has been driven out of schools, politics, and even out of theology! America is not far behind. The Middle East, however, has a firm unifying spiritual force in its commitment to Islam.

America in a Gilded Cage

The *Petroleum Economist* points an accusing finger at the American government for playing OPEC's game. At one time, President Nixon set as his goal "independence in energy by 1980." But that idea was soon forgotten. The *Petroleum Economist* laments our constantly greater dependence on the Middle East. America confirmed this dependence on May 15, 1978, nearly thirty years after the founding of Israel and its recognition by the United States. The U.S. Senate action was reported by *Nouvel Observateur*.

Recently, an ant crushed an elephant in Washington, according to the *New York Times*. Fourteen days earlier the *Times* had said that the Arab lobby was to the pro-Israel lobby as a fly is to a pachyderm. But now the Senate has rejected a resolution 54 to 44 for which pro-Israeli groups had mobilized all their followers and all their means. In question was the sale of fighter planes to Egypt and Saudi Arabia. This was the Israeli lobby's first defeat.

It would be wrong to saddle the Israeli prime minister with all the blame for this. Of course he made some wrong moves, but control had slipped from his hands. The "new realities" of economics, finance, and oil were determining factors for the Senate.

On the other hand, the Arab lobby is full of energy; important personalities have been mobilized: Bert Lance, John Connally, and William Fulbright among them. Joseph Baroody, one of the leaders of the Association of American Arabs, remarks gleefully, "People are beginning to listen to us! The Americans now want to see both sides of the coin."

On May 2 Sheik Yamani, Saudi Arabia's oil minister, issued his warning: Riyadh was willing and able to change its financial policies if the fighter planes were not delivered. King Khaled explained to a Kuwait newspaper the same day that he could also buy his planes "elsewhere." These official statements are couched in the most careful and moderate tones, but in private the Saudis are much sharper. The solidity of Ameri-

ca's friendship is deliberately being put to the
test.

More and more, discussions in the Senate center
on the Arab countries, and less and less on Israel.
Other issues which shove Israel into the background are the Soviets, Cuba, the energy crisis,
and other American interests. The pro-Israel
lobby simply cannot compete with all that.

This change of course is a victory for pragmatic
politics and the beginning of a new *Pax
Americana* in the Middle East, and this displeases
Israel. It is, by the way, by no means clear that
the general Arab population will be pleased for
very long with this situation. Who is the winner
in this battle, anyway? The Arab cause, the
Palestinians? Or, viewed in a sober light, American Big Business along with the most reactionary
governments in the Middle East?[9]

The U.S. Senate and the man on the street have both
opted for dependence on Arab oil rather than sacrificing comfort, luxury, and big cars. As distasteful as it
may seem, we must face squarely the question of
whether or not a nation that is dependent on imports
for half of its oil is justified in calling itself a world
power. America is caught in a gilded cage. The American fly can be sucked of its juices at any time by the
Arab spider.

The Arabs are buying U. S. Treasury securities,
especially the short-term type.[10] If they should dispose of them and other properties at one time, the
economy of the United States would totter and possi-

bly collapse. And the other nations of the West are in as precarious a position. Have the kings of the earth committed adultery with Babylon (see Rev. 18:3)?

The Last Race

"Today oil is the driving force of history," said Carlos Perez, the former president of Venezuela. Utopians believe that other energy sources will soon be found or other oil deposits discovered. But this race is lost before it has begun. Alaskan oil can only provide for ten to fifteen percent of America's need.

> North Sea oil simply offsets the over-consumption by America and Western Europe for the last two years. No industrial land is safe any longer from oil dependence. Whereas today foreign oil amounts to 50 percent of our needs, in 1973 it was only 10 percent. [11]

And while Alaskan oil does provide a small source for American oil consumption, Middle East oil is much easier to obtain.

> ARAMCO discovered a new oil field in 1969 containing about 8½ billion barrels. That is as much as the whole oil field on Prudhoe Bay, which was quite a sensation when it was discovered. While the Arctic cold necessitates great capital investments to build pipelines and heated conveyor equipment, the oil in the Middle East flows with its own pressure from deep in the desert, and can be pumped into ships without exorbitant costs. [12]

Between 1925 and 1929 the U.S. exported 69 percent of all the oil used in the world. Venezuela was second with 5.7 percent, followed by Mexico, the Soviet Union, Iran, and others. The total production in 1925 was 141 million tons. In 1973 the Arab world exported 1,222.4 million tons. The world oil reserve is estimated at 90 billion tons, of which 51 billion tons are in Arab lands.

The race for new energy has been lost. Assuming that more oil is found, we need about ten years to develop it and put it to use. And putting our hopes in atomic energy is like going down a one-way street. An article entitled "The Atomic Wager is a Pact which Faust is Making with the Devil" appeared in a 1974 periodical.

> To get out of the one-way street we are in, the world would have to build four nuclear reactors per week for a hundred years, which would cost two thousand billion dollars per year. To feed these reactors, 15 million kilos of plutonium 239 would have to be produced yearly. With certain precautionary measures the radioactive danger could be controlled. Breathing in ten micrograms is sufficient to cause fatal lung cancer.
>
> A ball of plutonium the size of a grapefruit contains enough poison to rid the earth of human life. The radioactivity of plutonium lasts for 25,000 years. [13]

What an apocalyptic picture! Our world is perched on the edge of an abyss. There is no escape other than selling out to the Arabs. Ishmael is in a very powerful position for its final battle with Isaac.

3

The Doctrine of Mohammed

It is no longer a secret that Islam has become actively engaged in an effort to convert the world to follow Allah. In 1974, at a meeting of the World Muslim League, an "Islamic World Mission Board" was formed. It was also decided that all Islamic universities would train missionaries to systematically spread Islamic doctrines.

In Mecca a powerful international radio station called the "Voice of Islam" is being built. One of its objectives is to scramble and drown out the Christian stations sending the gospel to Africa. There are about twenty-five Islamic radio corporations involved in this project.

Islam claims that Jesus and Moses were prophets and good men. And some Christians are beginning to claim they can worship with Moslems because "we worship the same god, only with different names." And yet if the god of the Moslems is the same as the God of the Christians, why is Islam so aggressively seeking converts and trying so hard to stamp out Christianity? Too often, we are allowing them to do it!

We are obviously not taking the Islamic missionary effort seriously enough; if we were, Christian churches would be more alarmed at what is happening. Christ has said that Christians are to be the salt of the world, but He warned of the salt losing its saltiness. Christ said Christians are to let their light shine before men, but we have hidden it. Christians have abandoned the authority of the written Word of God and of Jesus Christ in their lives and in their churches.

I am afraid most Christians today are too naive to see what is happening in the world. We don't recognize the Islamic threat for what it is. This ignorance makes us defenseless because we cannot see the consequences of the impending disaster. To understand our opposition, we will look at the background and nature of Islam, as well as its missionary and counter-Christian efforts today.

Mohammed

The founder of Islam, Mohammed, was born in A.D. 570 in the caravan town of Mecca in what is now Saudi Arabia. His father's name is said to have been Abdullah (servant of Allah), and he was one of the righteous men of his day. His mother's name was Amina, and both were members of the Quraish tribe. They were very poor, according to legend, because of their generosity.

Mohammed's father died before he was born, and his mother left him an orphan when he was six years old. Mohammed was brought up first by his grandfather and then by a likewise poor uncle who had many children. At an early age Mohammed had to learn to take care of himself, and he spent his teen-age years herding sheep and traveling with caravans through central Arabia, working as a camel driver and as the caravan master's orderly. These trips took him into Syria where he came into contact with Judaism and Christianity, both of which, in contrast to the pagan religions of Arabia, are monotheistic.

When he was twenty-five, Mohammed married Khadija, a wealthy widow fifteen years older than he was. With his new wealth, Mohammed left the caravan trade, became a merchant in Mecca, and spent much of his time in meditation. At the age of forty, Mohammed had a vision while he was alone in a cave three miles from Mecca, in which, he claimed, the angel Gabriel told him he was the messenger of Allah.

The Arabs of Mohammed's day worshiped many gods, and the center of the worship was the Kaaba in Mecca (still Islam's most holy place). The Kaaba is a stone structure that orthodox Moslems say has been built or rebuilt ten times. The current Kaaba, built in

Camel caravans, such as this, have traveled the same routes for four thousand years.

696, is forty feet by thirty-five feet by fifty feet high. In Mohammed's day 365 gods were worshiped in the Kaaba. Allah was one of these deities and the god of the Quraish tribe, of which Mohammed was a part. For four years after his vision, Mohammed proclaimed more and more openly that Allah was the *only* god and that he was Allah's prophet.

> When Mohammed was born in Mecca in 570, the black Kaaba Stone was the religious center of Arabia. In the great courtyard stood 365 idols. All types of deities were worshipped there. But the "true" god, the god of stone, surpassed them all in fame—it was the "god of gods"—and people were no longer offered to it, just animals. It was so mighty that it made Mecca unassailable.
>
> Mohammed drove the idols away; his god Allah was the only god. But he kept the Kaaba as a holy place and confirmed the power of the Black Stone to take away man's sins. He obligated every believer to make a pilgrimage to this holy place at least once in his lifetime (Koran: Sura 22:26-37).[1]

Mohammed's first convert was Khadija, his wife, and the second was his cousin Ali. Other converts were mostly slaves, and he was opposed as much for his welcoming slaves as he was for his religious beliefs. In 622, learning of a plot to kill him, Mohammed fled from Mecca to Yathrib—later renamed Medina—where he ruled until his death in 632.

Mohammed became the absolute ruler of Yath-

> rib where he founded his model theocratic state. He built the first mosque, changed the direction of prayers from Jerusalem to Mecca, and instituted the fast month of Ramadan and tithing. Relations with Christians and Jews deteriorated, but eventually he made treaties granting them freedom of worship in return for taxes.[2]

Mohammed's years in Yathrib were characterized by sixty-five campaigns and raids planned by him. In 630 he successfully conquered Mecca. The religion that now has visions of conquering the world was firmly established in the Arabian Desert.

Mohammed had all the characteristics of a false prophet. For instance, he claimed to be the last of the prophets and to have been the unique recipient of absolute truth. It is no wonder that the Jews considered him a false prophet, even in his own lifetime.

In Mecca some Jews saw little difference between the new faith of Mohammed and their own. In Medina, too, Mohammed was able to come to terms with the Jews.

> The Jews of Medina no longer liked this warlike faith, which had once seemed so flatteringly kindred to their own. They laughed at Mohammed's interpretation of their Scriptures and his claim to be the Messiah. . . . The Jews accused him of returning to idolatry.[3]

By comparing his claims with the New Testament—God's ultimate revealed truth—thinking Christians can easily expose these claims as false.

The Kaaba. Located in Mecca, it is the most important of Islamic holy places and the cradle of Islam. According to Islamic beliefs, the "Black Stone" has the power to take away sins when one kisses it. Even before Mohammed's time it was worshipped as the "god of stone" and was but one of 365 gods honored there.

Mohammed claimed to have his call and the new truth in the Koran revealed to him from Allah through the angel Gabriel. And yet God says, "And we know that the Son of God has come and has given us an understanding, that we may know Him who is true; and we are in Him who is true, in His Son Jesus Christ. This is the true God and eternal life" (1 John 5:20).

Mohammed claimed that "there is no god but Allah, and Mohammed is the Prophet of Allah" (This is the Islamic creed called the *Kalima*). And yet God says, "For there is one God and one Mediator between God and men, the Man Christ Jesus, who gave Himself a ransom for all . . ." (1 Tim. 2:5,6).

Mohammed claimed that eternal life depended on a

person's moral behavior. All good Muslims are to perform the religious duties called the "Five Pillars of Islam":

a) recitation of the *Kalima* aloud, correctly, and with full understanding;

b) praying five times daily—at dawn, noon, afternoon, evening, and night—bowing toward Mecca;

c) giving alms for religious purposes and to help the poor and the sick;

d) fasting during the daytime for the month of Ramadan, and

e) making a pilgrimage to Mecca at least once in a person's lifetime.

And yet God says, " 'And this is eternal life, that they may know You, the only true God, and Jesus Christ whom You have sent' " (John 17:3).

It is clear from these passages that no one can know God except through Jesus Christ. Only His perfect sacrifice opens the way to God and brings forgiveness, inner peace, and eternal life. " 'Nor is there salvation in any other, for there is no other name under heaven given among men by which we must be saved' " (Acts 4:12).

Allah

Before Mohammed's birth, his father had spoken the magic word *Bismillah* ("in the name of Allah") to put Amina's expected child under the protection of Allah, one of the 365 deities worshiped in the Kaaba and the god of the Quraish tribe. Thus Mohammed was dedicated before his birth to the god of a religion whose founder he was to become. Although Allah displaced the 364 other idols of the Kaaba, he remains a false god.

> Even before Mohammed, a heathen demon was worshipped in the Kaaba in Mecca. At a heathen sacrificial feast in that city, Mohammed stood up, pointed to the Kaaba stone, and cried, "La alla illa allahu!" ("There is no allah, except he be Allah.") This utterance of Mohammed's, changed into "La illahilla Allah" ("There is no God but Allah"), became the Islamic confession of faith.

> The Kaaba was the first Islamic holy place. The actual nucleus of Islam lies in this commitment to Allah, the highest demon. Those who commit themselves to this spirit become prisoners of Satan.

> Islam is therefore a religion which must always turn against Jesus Christ, the crucified, risen, coming Lord. It is an expressly anti-Christian religion of lies, boundless fatalism, and unimaginable fanaticism. [4]

As pictured in the Koran, the holy book of Islam, Allah is a soulless, rigid god who shows no mercy. To him man is simply a slave, having no power of decision. Allah demands the total submission of all creatures. He is selfishness taken to its logical extreme, a gruesome tyrant who can only give commands. Faith in such a god can lead only to a dismal fatalism.

Allah is not a god who revealed himself, but a god who was given a unique position by Mohammed.

Mohammed chose Allah from among the 365 gods
being worshiped in the Kaaba. Even today pilgrims
going to Mecca bow to the spirit who inhabited the
Kaaba long before Islam. According to Islam, whoever
kisses the Kaaba stone experiences forgiveness of sin
and may perhaps go to paradise when he dies. In
contrast, the Scriptures teach,

> Before Me there was no God formed,
> And there will be none after Me.
> I, even I, am the LORD;
> And there is no savior besides Me.
> (Is. 43:10,11)

Is Allah the God of the Bible?

> We are not living in error because the truth is
> hard to understand—often it is near enough to
> touch—but because error is more comfortable.
> —Aleksandr Solzhenitsyn

In many areas of life a spirit of toleration is an
admirable trait. And yet we in the West are letting a
spirit of toleration encourage us to accept error as
truth. One example is the idea that Allah and Jehovah
(the self-revealing God of the Old and New Testaments) are one and the same deity. This idea is even
promoted, for instance, in the Roman Catholic publication *One God—All Brothers*. But nothing could be
farther from the truth.

This lie seems to be endorsed by the Koran.

> They say, moreover, "Become Jews or Christians
> that ye may have the *true* guidance." SAY: Nay!

THE DOCTRINE OF MOHAMMED

the religion of Abraham, the sound in faith, and not one of those who join gods with God (sura 2:129)!

And the credo of Islam is:

Say ye: "We believe in God, and that which hath been sent down to us, and that which hath been sent down to Abraham and Ismael and Isaac and Jacob and the tribes: and that which hath been given to Moses and to Jesus, and that which was given to the prophets from their Lord. No difference do we make between any of them: and to God are we resigned (Muslims)" (sura 2:130).

The Old Testament clearly teaches that ". . . The LORD is our God, the LORD is one" (Deut. 6:4)! And yet this doctrine of the oneness of God has been degraded by Mohammed, and the idea of the Trinity blindly misunderstood and denied. Dr. John Alden Williams explains the Islamic position.

Jesus holds a unique place among the prophets in Islam. He is born of a virgin "purified above all women," he is the promised Messiah, "The Word of God and a Spirit from Him," an almost superhuman figure who spoke from the cradle and worked great wonders by the power of God; but the central doctrines of Christianity are set aside. The idea that he is the Son of God is sternly rejected, the doctrine of the Trinity is held to contradict God's Oneness. . . . The early Christians are held to have deliberately falsified the scripture he brought, and to have worshipped the Messiah blasphemously. Later genera-

> tions have been perhaps sincere but certainly
> misguided, so that a new revelation became
> necessary. As for Jesus, God took him to Himself
> when the Jews rejected him (without Jesus'
> being crucified), and will justify him before the
> end of the world.[5]

The Son of God became flesh and gave us a complete revelation of the eternal God. There is only one true, living God, who unites in His being three divine Persons: Father, Son, and Holy Spirit. Such a mystery could never have been revealed by human reason alone. The triune God can be known only by faith, through Jesus Christ. Jehovah—the God of the Old and New Testaments—is the one true living God, the eternal Father; and by comparing His character and nature with that of Allah, we can easily see what a poor imitation Allah is.

It is true that Judaism, Christianity, and Islam are monotheistic religions.

> There are only three monotheistic religions:
> Judaism, Christianity, and Islam. All the others
> have many gods—with the exception of Budd-
> hism, which has no god. Judaism was the first
> monotheistic religion. God revealed Himself to
> Abraham, who became the first believer in a
> consistent monotheistic faith.[6]

Monotheism is certainly the only form of religion compatible with our modern Western mentality. If we start logically with God the Creator, whom we conceive as only one, there is no place for a family of gods.

It is interesting, though, that the great majority of peoples are polytheistic. I believe that all religions with many gods (they are actually idols) originate not in revelation from God but from satanic influences. There is hardly anything so repulsive to Satan as the fact that there is only one God, omniscient and omnipotent, the only Ruler, to whom belongs all honor and obedience. The devil has always revolted against the truth. He tries to obscure it continually and with every means at his disposal, but never with total success. Therefore he promotes the idea of many gods.

The ancient Greeks had many gods, and when the apostle Paul found an altar in Athens with the inscription "To an Unknown God," he immediately saw a point of contact: " 'the One whom you worship without knowing, Him I proclaim to you' " (Acts 17:23). As long as one believes in only one god, he is at least right in his fundamental concept of God, even though he may not know Him and may have errors in his understanding of the nature and character of God.

Followers of Mohammed believe in one god, but not the God of the Bible. One of the most important areas of difference is the Christian's belief in a triune God.

A model of trinity is found in man himself, who was created in God's image, and consists of body, soul, and spirit. God is love. In Him is the fullness of love from eternity to eternity. Man is ordained to a life of love, unfolding in its fullness in the relationship I—you—He.

The plural name for God, *Elohim*, which frequently appears in the first chapters of the Bible, points to the

Holy Trinity. Creation itself could be seen as an act of love, with God saying " 'Let *Us* make man in *Our* image . . .' " (Gen. 1:26, italics added).

Since the concept of a Holy Trinity puzzles most people, including Christians, let us examine the doctrine. The New Testament speaks clearly of the Father, the Son, and the Holy Spirit. Further, it is clear that the divine qualities of omnipotence, omnipresence, omniscience, and eternal existence are ascribed to all three Persons. This is why Jews and Moslems reproach Christians for having forsaken the correct view: There is only one God.

Jesus Himself cited as the first commandment, " '. . . Hear, O Israel, the LORD our God is one LORD; And you shall love the LORD your God with all your heart, with all your soul, with all your mind, and with all your strength . . .' " (Mark 12:29,30). In Isaiah 44:6 we read, " '. . . I am the first and I am the last,/And there is no God besides me.' "

Jews and Moslems will not allow for a God who is one but who exists eternally in three Persons. We must admit that the word *Trinity* is not in the Bible, but the reality of the Trinity is pervasive from Genesis to Revelation. There are passages in which the three Persons are named in succession: ". . . baptizing them in the name of the Father and of the Son and of the Holy Spirit" (Matt. 28:19); " 'I will pray the Father, and He will give you another Helper, that He may abide with you forever, even the Spirit of truth . . .' " (John 14:16,17).

It is noteworthy that even in the Old Testament God speaks of Himself in the plural: " 'Let Us make man . . .'' (Gen. 1:26); ". . . 'the man has become like one of

Us, knowing good and evil . . .' " (Gen. 3:22); ". . . 'Whom shall I send, and who will go for Us? . . .' " (Is. 6:8). Thus, along with the strong emphasis on only one God, we find several passages in the Old Testament speaking of God in the plural.

Dr. Nathan Wood says that the world in which we live is God's handiwork, and therefore the creation should reflect the character of the Creator. If God is only one, but reveals Himself to us in three eternal Persons, we should be able to find parallels to this in nature.

Let us begin with time. There is only one "time." No one has ever suggested otherwise. We perceive it, however, in three aspects: past, present, and future. All three are in our mind when we reflect on the concept of time.

Closely related is the idea of space. There is only one "space." Yet it is unthinkable without three dimensions. No one dimension exists alone, and all three are necessary.

Or think of man himself. Each of us is an independent creature, self-contained, yet the Bible teaches that we consist of body, soul, and spirit. Body alone makes no person, and certainly not spirit alone. Only the three together can make a person.

Lastly, think of matter. We find it in three states: solid, liquid, and gas. The most well-known example of course is ice, water, and steam: The same substance, but with three clearly differentiated forms.[7]

None of these examples proves the Trinity, but they help us understand "three-in-oneness" and see that the triune God is reflected in His creation.

God is not the God of Abraham, *Ishmael*, and Jacob,

but of Abraham, *Isaac,* and Jacob. The followers of Mohammed accuse Isaac of not being the true son, but it was Ishmael—not Isaac—who was cast out. God said to Abraham, " 'My covenant will I establish with Isaac, whom Sarah will bear . . .' " (Gen. 17:21). God gave promises to Ishmael for Abraham's sake, but He entered into no convenant with Ishmael's line.

The late missionary Robert H. Glover observed that the god of Islam, "far from being the loving and beneficient God of the Christian Bible, is an unfeeling despot, infinitely removed from His creatures, with no mediator between."[8] Allah has nothing to do with the God of the Bible. He is a poor counterfeit of God. *It is blasphemy to put Allah and Jehovah on the same level.*

The Koran

Islam was founded by Mohammed, its god is Allah, and its holy book is the Koran. According to Moslems, the original of the Koran is in heaven in the Arabic language—the language of Allah and therefore the most perfect, complete language of all. The Koran was not translated into other languages for a long time in order to prevent this divine language from being desecrated. But today it is translated and distributed widely to make Allah's teachings accessible to all men.

The word "Koran" means "reading," and Moslems say that the book was dictated to Mohammed by the angel Gabriel. During the last twenty-three years of his life, Mohammed spoke various portions of the Koran, which were written down by his followers. These portions were kept in various places with no attempt made to put them in logical or chronological order. After Mohammed's death, many of the owners of the fragments were killed in battle, and there was some danger that the words of Mohammed would be lost. Omar, caliph of Abu Bakr, commissioned Zaid ibn Thabit, who had been Mohammed's secretary, to collect the sayings. The result was the Koran.

The Koran consists of 114 chapters called *suras*. After the opening sura, they are generally arranged in order of decreasing length. Since earlier utterances tended to be shorter, the Koran is more or less in reverse chronological order. Except for sura 9, each chapter begins with "In the Name of God, the Compassionate, the Merciful."

Just as Allah is a counterfeit of God, the Koran is a counterfeit of the Bible. In order to be able to discern truth and recognize lies, we must ally ourselves with the apostles and prophets in recognizing Jesus Christ as the cornerstone of our faith and the Bible as the inspired Word of God and our highest written authority. Unfortunately, some Western Christians have started to waver, forsaking and ignoring this God-breathed authority. Therefore, Qaddafi of Libya can say,

> Christianity must consist of many question marks. It has absolutely no divine message. It has always been a tool of imperialism and allied with capitalistic exploiters. Islam is the only valid religion, encompassing all others. Jesus was a Moslem—he has more connections with us than with Christianity.[9]

The apostle Paul clearly stated, "But even if we, or an angel from heaven, preach any other gospel to you

An African Faki *(an Islamic scribe) studying the Koran.*

than what we have preached to you, let him be accursed" (Gal. 1:8). The message of the Koran is clearly "another gospel" from that of the apostles, and yet the Muslims frequently treat it with more reverence than Christians treat the Bible.

While my family and I were still in Africa, we would often be awakened early whenever we slept near an Arab village. African children would be sitting around a fire with the *faki*, or scribe, learning the Koran by heart. Every young Arab is proud to learn and recite verses from the Koran and sometimes seven- or eight-year-old boys can recite the whole Koran without a mistake! It is their first reader, and it becomes the only world they know, with all its rules and regulations. Its formative influence on the people can hardly be overestimated. Every time I entered an Arab village, the *faki* would be sitting in the shade of a mimosa tree, willing to read from the Koran to anyone who would sit down with him.

There are very beautiful editions of the Koran with intricate first letters of chapters and other designs. One even finds pages of decorative text on the walls of huts or on the cabs of trucks. Koran verses are also worn around the neck as charms; many Africans do this who are not yet "Mohammedans," but who believe in the power of the "holy book." More and more people, especially in black Africa, are being drawn under the spell of the Koran and its god.

The Chosen People

As taught in the Koran, Islam is the only true religion. In fact, Mohammed lays claim for his followers to the promises which God gave Israel in Deuteronomy 14:2. God said to the children of Israel, " '. . . the Lord has chosen you to be a people for His own possession out of all the peoples who are on the face of the earth.' " Mohammed, however, said to his followers in the Koran:

> Ye are the best folk that hath been raised up unto mankind. Ye enjoin the Just, and ye forbid the Evil, and ye believe in God: And if the people of the Book [the Jews] had believed it had surely been better for them! Believers there are among them, but most of them are perverse (sura 3:106).

Mohammed claims the uniqueness for his followers that God gave to the Jews because, on one hand, he injected into his teachings the poison of hatred for Jews and Christians. That hatred has not lost its potency through the centuries. He cursed the Jews in the name of Allah (Koran, sura 4:42–55), preached hatred and damnation on all who will not accept Islam, and urged his followers not to have any dealings with Jews or Christians.

> O Believers! take not the Jews or Christians as friends. They are but one another's friends. If any one of you taketh them for his friends, he surely is one of them! God will not guide the evil doers (sura 5:56).

On the other hand, Islam claims that Christians and Jews are really Moslems. Qaddafi made this very clear in a speech in Cairo.

> Many believe that Moslems are simply the followers of the prophet Mohammed. This is wrong according to the Koran, which claims that the followers of all the monotheistic religions mentioned in the holy book of Koran are Moslems. All those who have believed in one God were Moslems, even before Mohammed. That is doubtless the *divine* view of Islam. On this point we read in the Koran:
> "To be repeated: We believe in God, in the revelation given us, in Abraham, Ishmael, Isaac, Jacob, and the tribes, in the revelation given to Moses and Jesus and the prophets. We do not distinguish between one or the other, we submit ourselves to God in Islam."
> It is clear from this verse that there is no difference between Jesus, Moses, Mohammed, Abraham, Isaac, Jacob, or Ishmael, for they were all

Moslems. All Moslems are obliged to believe in all the prophets in the Koran. So there is no reason to distinguish between them; this is true monotheism. God created all peoples and is the Lord of the universe.

Thus we believe it to be our duty to enlighten Jews and Christians. The verse I quoted mentioned salvation and redemption for all who believe in what Mohammed believed. If a Christian should defend the truth of this verse, he would find himself in contradiction to his own faith. He would have to change his view to remain a true believer; if not, he would be judged for his sins on resurrection day and have to do penance.

The concept "divine" in Islam means the calling of all men to Islam. Every prophet since the very first one has repeated this call. Mohammed was the last of these prophets; he ends the long line of descent of the prophets.

The logical conclusion is that Islam replaces all the teachings of the apostles. In Islam one must renounce any distinction between believers in Mohammed, Jesus, or any other apostle.

Whoever finds himself in error must be brought back to the right path. The Koran never commanded that we fight among ourselves to determine who is right and who is wrong. As long as our belief in God is the main standard in settling differences of opinion, we will always successfully come to an understanding.

> If you agree with this *divine* conception of religion, no one will think of using force to solve differences, for Islam, just as Christianity, rejects violence.[10]

One must give Qaddafi credit for stating things so clearly that there can be no misunderstanding. Contemporary Islam has no intention of building bridges to Christianity. No "peaceful coexistence" here! It is a law of nature that the weak should submit to the strong, and Islam does not view itself as weak. Islam is a religion of natural man and his god, and it cannot recognize any other set of laws. Followers of Mohammed see themselves as being chosen by Allah to dominate the world. The promises given by God to the children of Israel are being claimed by the children of Ishmael.

Mohammed and Christ

Mohammedans have subjugated innumerable people and races and made allies of them: Syrians, Egyptians, Berbers, Persians, Nubians. In the seventh century Islam spread across the whole North African coast through wars and trade. Whoever accepted Islam was on the side of the victors and could look confidently to the future.

The Jews could not be assimilated because the power of their beliefs withstood the onslaught of Islam. They rejected Mohammed from the very beginning because they saw that he was preaching ideas that were contrary to the Bible. Likewise, Mohammed and Christ are incompatible. For instance, one becomes a follower of Mohammed by saying, "There is no God but Allah, and Mohammed is his prophet."

In contrast, one becomes a Christian through the work of the Holy Spirit in the heart. Through belief in Jesus Christ, the Son of God, and His death on the cross, a person becomes a child of God and his sins are forgiven. A follower of Mohammed achieves eternal life by performing religious duties, but a Christian enters into a relationship with God and receives eternal life as a gift. The first Christians believed this, and many went to their deaths because of the faith. Our fathers believed this, and so do all who take the Bible seriously. " '. . . I believe that Jesus Christ is the Son of God' " (Acts 8:37) was the confession of the treasury official from Ethiopia. Peter's confession was, ". . .'You are the Christ, the Son of the living God" (Matt. 16:16). Paul, the apostle to the Gentiles, made it clear that everyone who accepted the message of the crucified Christ received the seal of the Holy Spirit and became a member of the body of Christ.

> In Him you also trusted, after you heard the word of truth, the gospel of your salvation; in whom also, having believed, you were sealed with the Holy Spirit of promise, who is the guarantee of our inheritance until the redemption of the purchased possession, to the praise of His glory (Eph. 1:13,14).

According to the Koran's teachings, however, the promised spirit mentioned in the New Testament is Mohammed.

In his teaching Jesus repeatedly emphasized that

salvation came through Isaac's line. He never mentioned the line of Ishmael as being the vehicle of God's salvation (see Matt. 22:32, Mark 12:26, Luke 20:37). Jesus said to the Samaritan woman, " 'You worship what you do not know; we know what we worship, for salvation is of the Jews' " (John 4:22). Jesus emphasized that salvation is available only through Himself, from the line of Abraham, Isaac, and Jacob. Stephen, the first Christian martyr, spoke of the God of Abraham, Isaac, and Jacob, and this testimony cost him his life. How many Christians today would be willing to lay down their lives for Stephen's God? Today the West is bowing to the children of Ishmael simply to survive.

A New Holy War

In addition to the five pillars of Islam mentioned earlier, the Koran also teaches a sixth: *jihad,* or holy war. Mohammed tried to win converts by persuasion, but when that failed he encouraged the use of force in securing converts. The sword was considered a valid instrument for spreading Islam throughout the world. If any of his followers were killed in a holy war, Mohammed promised that they would go to paradise. Ayatollah Khomeini reiterates this: "If you are slain, you will go to paradise. Even if you do the slaying, you will go to paradise. That is Islamic logic!" And yet Christ said, " 'all who take the sword will perish by the sword' " (Matt. 26:52).

Holy wars were common in the years after Mohammed's death. All of northern Africa and much of Spain came under Islamic influence this way in the seventh century. The Arab commander-in-chief El Okbar conquered all of North Africa. When he reached the Atlantic, he rode his horse out into the water, drew his sword, and cried, *"Bismellahi!* If the ocean were not in my way, I would carry the prophet's message even farther west!" After the defeat of the Islamic armies by Charles Martel at Tours in central France, Islam looked eastward conquering India, Java, the Philippines, and other countries. The idea of a holy war has not been strongly preached this century until recently when many of the older Islamic customs were revived.

One Islamic country after another, for instance, is changing its laws to bring them into accord with the *sharia,* the laws of the Koran. In February, 1979, it was Pakistan; now it's Iran, and soon it will be Turkey. They are all restructuring their society according to the ideal state described by Mohammed. All Christian influence, stemming from the colonial era, is being systematically purged. Old laws are being reintroduced.

Thieves have their hand or foot cut off, adulteresses are stoned to death, a drink of alcohol or any publicly offensive act brings a whipping. These laws are not applied to followers of Mohammed only, but to foreign workers in the Middle East as well.

Today after the millennial sleep that almost led to its death, Islam seems to be realizing the dream of the seventh-century general El Okbar. Before 1970, Arab nationalism was more open to Western culture and sometimes even tried to identify with it. Now that is past. The Islamic revolution is in motion, and it has the goal of conquering the world.

> Only he can wear the mantle of the prophet who is in position to defend Islam by the sword throughout the world.[11]

4

The Islamic Reawakening

A new era has begun, both for the world in general and for Islam itself. Islam is no longer subservient to and tolerant of others. It is a different Islam, accusing Christians and Jews of being heretics, worse than heathen. Islam is declaring war on anyone who gets in its way. Free-thinkers, atheists, Christians, Jews, non-Islamic missionaries, and apostate Moslems are regarded as "foreign bodies" to be rejected or annihilated. It is a totalitarian religion, claiming a right to religious as well as political dominion throughout the world.

Persecution, war, and animosity are a heritage from the past for Moslems. As we approach the end of time Moslems will become more intense worldwide. They will become enmity against God, His Anointed, and the people of Israel.

Of the blessing which Allah supposedly sends flowing from the Arabian desert, he retains a percentage for himself. It is reported that nearly five percent of all this land's income is used for the holy war. What enormous resources are at the disposal of Allah's soldiers! They have the means to wage war worldwide—militarily, ideologically, and economically.

And they will do this with revolutionary fervor. The summons to the holy war is being given against the unfaithful, the godless, and the people of promise—Israel.

> For twenty years the call went out from the Dome of the Rock for the destruction of Israel. In our day, after the removal of the dividing wall between the old and new city by the Israelis, the same summons is heard from the same mosque for the same holy war. From the same place where the holy place of Israel was once destroyed, a "final solution" is being called for. Can that be the "abomination of desolation" of which Jesus and the prophets spoke? Right where the God of Israel had His dwelling-place, followers of the "false prophet" are calling for annihilation of God's people.
>
> On June 2, 1967, Ahmed Choukeiri did just that, saying, "To Allah be honor at this moment when we are preparing to enter into a holy war to liberate Palestine and purge the holy land of the unfaithful and godless."[1]

A new threat arose when in July, 1980, the Israeli Knesset declared that undivided Jerusalem would be that country's eternal capital. Almost immediately Saudi Arabia's Crown Prince Fahd called for a holy war against Israel.

Islam is experiencing a reformation, and more and more of the 650 million Moslems are submitting completely to the laws of the Koran. They are ready and anxious to join in a holy war against all their enemies —Jews, unbelievers, and Christians.

Mosque in Istanbul.

Christians in Danger

In country after country around the world, Christians are either being oppressed or they are simply tolerated and are a quickly disappearing minority. Islam is gaining in strength and militancy. Many Islamic countries are ruled by totalitarian laws, and no ideology is permitted other than the state religion. But this doesn't stop the Muslims from boasting of unparalleled tolerance. A Swiss newspaper commented on this situation.

> It would be a misrepresentation of history to claim that Arab conquests had not forced Islam on the conquered peoples; it simply does not correspond to the facts. Exacting research points to the opposite.

> Mohammed himself began, especially in his last years, to spread his faith by the sword, making converts by force. He was especially severe in his attacks on Jewish settlements in Arabia. Again and again he sought pretexts upon which to banish or exterminate the Jews.

> At this time, the so-called Holy War began which has lasted through the centuries. While the prophet was especially hostile and vengeful toward unbelievers and other adversaries, anyone who accepted Islam became his brother without further ceremony. Later came the campaigns of the Seljuks and the persecutions of Jews and Christians in North Africa and Spain. Such things were still going on at the beginning of our century. The Armenians, an ancient

Christian people, would not accept the Koran and were driven from their homeland of centuries by the Turks in a cold-blooded, vicious manner. The men were driven into the desert to die of hunger or thirst, women and girls were raped and sold to harems.

When in exceptional cases, usually for political or commercial reasons, Christians or Jews were tolerated in Muslim lands, they belonged to an outlawed class with no possibility of holding an office of any kind. They were exploited and oppressed with every possible means, and burdened with extra taxes. At the best, their life was one of quiet resignation.

Whoever has studied the Koran knows that the very essence of Islam makes it the most intolerant of all religions. The Koran itself says:

> O ye true believers! Do not become friendly with Jews or Christians! Kill the idol-worshippers wherever you find them, take them prisoner, besiege them, lie in wait for them. When you meet unbelievers, cut their heads off, make a bloodbath out of it.[2]

Let's see what the current situation is and how Christians are being treated in various Moslem countries.*

---

*Statistical information in this section is quoted from *The World Almanac & Book of Facts*, 1980 (New York: Newspaper Enterprise Association, Inc., 1979).

In *Syria* (population 8,100,000; 71,498 square miles) the political situation is particularly uncertain. Not a week goes by but extremist Moslems or followers of the Iraqi Baath Party make an attempt on the life of President Assad. When one considers that more than half of all American and French weapons exports are to the Middle East, one can only fear the worst.

In *Turkey* (population 43,210,000; 301,380 square miles) hatred of Christians is being strengthened by the troubles in Lebanon. Many Kurds are unemployed; they are forming armed bands, robbing cattle, and destroying the fruit crops of Christian villages, as well as ambushing and murdering Christian farmers.

In the eastern part of Mardin, a province of Turkey, there were many villages where Christians and Moslems dwelt peacefully together; but now the Christians are beginning to flee. For example, in the village of Azech, where Christians were the majority a decade ago, most of the Christians have gone.

The Turkish Premier Suleyman Demirel has never really dealt with the grievances in Turkey's poor southeast. As in Lebanon, radical political groups with volatile emotions in the province of Mardin are stirring up sentiment against the Christians. Demirel has been soft on the fanatic Moslems, and so it is no wonder so many Christians, oppressed by armed Moslem gangs, are leaving their villages in Tur-Abdin.

With the cry, "Turkey for the Moslems!", women and children are being murdered and men castrated (a measure taken by soldiers in a "holy war" so that their victims will have no sexual temptations in the afterlife) before they are killed. President Bulent Ecevit reportedly has said that it is a case of genuine whole-sale murder.

In Turkey there have been more victims than in Iran, but the press has not reported it.

In *Indonesia* (population 143,280,000; 735,268 square miles), the ten percent of the population who are Christians are an important factor in the nation. Their schools, hospitals, and other social-assistance works are open to all. Due to their good education, they are found in every responsible position. But most of the population is Moslem, and a militant minority wants to make Indonesia a Moslem state. Islam's assault has gained momentum recently, and it is making political headway. Thus, religious freedom is continuously threatened.

Islam is the state religion of *Egypt* (population 39,640,000; 363,250 square miles). It is painful to realize that the land in the forefront for national eman-cipation and economic independence is also the land where native Christian congregations and missions are being the most severely tested. They live in great uncertainty. The Coptic Christians, whose church dates back to the time of the apostles, are not recog-nized as Egyptians by the government. Recent laws force foreign business concerns to hire natives as eighty percent of their personnel. And Christians are not considered natives, so many of them have no work. "Pure" Egyptians, i.e. Muslims, are hired in their place. Other tricks and death threats are being used on our Christian brothers in the Nile valley.

Christians in the *Sudan* (population 16,950,000; 967,491 square miles) are under pressure if not persecution. Islam is being forced on the country by Saudi Arabia and other oil-rich lands, not just as another religion, but as the state religion. The goal is the total Islamization of the Sudan.

After two years of intense activity in the *Comoro Islands* (population 370,000; 693 square miles) the Africa Inland Mission was ordered to withdraw all its missionaries from the island republic. The Moslem government arrested two missionaries and declared the other sixteen to be *persona non grata* in reaction to the spread of the gospel in the islands.

In *Morocco* (population 18,910,000; 171,953 square miles) a physician named Campbell had worked in a clinic in Safi, a city on the Atlantic, for five years and had made enough contact with the people so that some had become Christians. His successful efforts to bring people to Christ were considered illegal, and although he was not thrown into prison, he was forced to leave the country very quickly. He left behind him a group of baptized former Muslims. The believers are not permitted to have meetings, but they know well who is a fellow Christian. One can hope and pray that they are being spiritually fed.

Iraq (population 12,330,000; 172,000 square miles) is also an Islamic state. Six hundred Christians have been arrested there since November, 1978, among them some foreigners. Only four percent of the population lists itself as Christian. [At the time of publication of this edition in fall 1980, Iraq is waging a fierce border war with Iran—Editor.]

The *Yemen Arab Republic* (population 7,080,000; 75,289 square miles) and the *People's Democratic Republic of Yemen* (population 1,801,000; 112,000 square miles) are both located on the southern tip of the Arabian Peninsula on the Red Sea. In early 1979 all members of the Evangelical Mission had to leave Yemen after they were forced to sign a statement that they would not talk about Christ or distribute literature anymore

Jesus Christ is described as a prophet in the Koran, but Moslems still forbid missionaries to talk of Him or distribute literature. It is interesting that Islamic missions in Europe are under no such restrictions; they are free to distribute their literature and spread the doctrines of the Koran.

Afghanistan (population 17,450,000; 260,000 square miles) is a Moslem state.

> The Afghan state banned Armenian Christians and Jews from its territory back in 1926. It Islamized a former Hindu province, and changed its name from Kafiristan (land of blasphemers) to Nourestan (land of light).[3]

The Afghan government decreed the destruction of the only Christian church in the country, and on July 15, 1974, it was razed by a bulldozer. The American pastor had been forced to leave three months before. Permission to build the church had been granted to the Kabul congregation in 1959 during a visit by U.S. President Dwight Eisenhower. This church was destroyed at the very time a mosque was being built in Hollywood, California.

In *Chad* (population 4,310,000; 495,752 square miles), the largest mosque in Black Africa and an Islamic university have been built in the capital, N-Djamena. Islam has gained a foothold south of the

Sahara Desert. For every convert to Christianity in Africa, there are nine converts to Islam. Black Africa is being strewn with mosques, gifts to the poorer peoples of the Third World from the Persian Gulf states or Libya.

In *Tunisia* (population 6,220,000; 63,378 square miles) there are presently very few native Christians, perhaps twenty-five. Although the regime is politically quite tolerant, it is very difficult for these believers to gather together. Missionary activity is strictly forbidden. The interpretation of the United Nations' Charter with respect to religious freedom is rather peculiar. One is free to be a Christian or a Muslim, but as a Muslim one is forbidden to change his religion!

The largest mosque in Black Africa, N'Djamena, Chad. For every one convert to Christianity in Africa there are nine converts to Islam. Mosques are literally being stewn across Black Africa, gifts to the poor peoples of the Third World from Islamic nations.

In *Libya* (population 2,430,000; 679,536 square miles), the apparent leader in the Muslim awakening, Islam has been raised to the status of a state ideology. Every action and attitude of the citizen is to be tested by the question, "Would the Prophet approve of this action or attitude?"

Everything coming from overseas—customs, philosophy, literature, culture, religion—is refused or destroyed. The "contamination of the Moslem way of thinking" must stop. The Prophet gave the Arabs, and through them the whole world, the word of Allah. Nothing else may be placed above or even next to it.

The Renaissance of Islam

In countries where Islam is in control, Christians are second-class citizens at best. They are expected to obey Islamic laws, which govern all activities of life. Yet while Christian missions are being forced to suspend work in Moslem lands and churches are being made into mosques, Islam is building mosques in Christian lands. Not even the pope had the power to prevent the construction of a mosque and an Islamic university in Rome, overlooking St. Peter's from its spot high on Monte Mario. Qaddafi is helping with the construction costs by providing $10 million and Saudi Arabia is giving $20 million. The West is being prepared for the spread of Islam.

The Christian world is allowing itself to be led astray by measuring Islam by Western standards. And yet the Islamic brand of fanaticism is something we find difficult to understand.

Islam is totalitarian. It not only refuses non-Muslims religious freedom, but recognizing other religions as legitimate is for Muslims themselves unthinkable. There is no doubt allowed regarding Islam's qualifications as the only true religion. One god, one religion—a true Muslim cannot be dissuaded from this view.[4]

Islam is currently waging a war against unbelievers in Islamic lands, and it is pushing into the Far East and the South Pacific where it has reached New Guinea. Wherever it is already established, it is strengthening its foothold. In Africa whole tribes and villages have been converted to Islam. The economic promises that Islamic countries can now make to their poorer African neighbors increase their power and influence.

The gradual awakening of Islam in this century is taking place outwardly in the form of geographical expansion and inwardly in the form of a renaissance of the religious and cultural values of the classical Islamic civilization of the Middle Ages. Islam is making steady inroads into Africa. Colonel Qaddafi, spark-plug of the Arab unity movement and a figure around whom all progressives rally in the Muslim world, said, "The African continent must become Islamic."[5]

Just as in Africa, Islam is making inroads in Europe, although it seems outwardly to be quite inconspicuous and harmless. In England, France, and Sweden, the Muslims are already the second largest religious body. In Yugoslavia since World War II, six hundred new mosques have been built, partly subsidized by the state. On the other hand, Christian churches seem to become less and less important.

There are a tremendous number of people from Islamic countries working in Europe today. They are attracted by the availability of jobs and high pay. In 1974 an article entitled, "Islam on a Gigantic March to the West—Last Warning to Christians," said:

> The North Africans working in France and the Turks in Germany and the rest of Central Europe may become infiltrators without necessarily realizing it. Are they the Trojan Horse, to be used by the Arabs when they decide to reach for the southern shores of Europe? Are these foreign workers indeed—perhaps in the coming generation—the fifth column?

The mosque in Paris. At the dedication of the mosque, the message of the Second Vatican Council was stressed: [The church] "looks with respect upon Mohammedans, since they believe in God." In France there are two Muslims to every Protestant.

> While more and more churches in North Africa
> are being transformed into mosques, more and
> more mosques are appearing in Europe, while
> many churches, on the other hand, are becoming
> night spots for dancing.
>
> The oil sheiks are buying up whole blocks in
> European cities, as well as large areas of real
> estate. With nearly unlimited capital, they are
> now involved in big industry and will one day
> have the final say regarding the future of our
> industrial production.
>
> No Mohammedan becomes a Christian by min-
> gling with or marrying a European, but more
> and more Christian women are becoming Mus-
> lims through marriage to a Mohammedan, and
> the children become Muslims.[6]

Let's look at some developments in various European countries to see how Islam is spreading its influence.

On September 17, 1976, the first mosque in Alsace,
France, was dedicated at St. Louis. To show their good
will and unity, various authorities were present including Monsignor Elchinger of Strasbourg. A
speaker stressed the meaning of the Second Vatican
Council and referred to the fact that "the Church looks
upon Mohammedans with respect, since they believe
in God."

The mosque in St. Louis was only the beginning, for
at the dedication, the "Association Musulmane" of
Alsace asked for support in building a mosque in the

near future in Mulhouse. Because of the many foreign workers, there are now two Muslims for every Protestant in France.

In *Spain*, the descendants of the Muslim settlers of Andalusia feel drawn again to this area. It was Muslim for nearly eight hundred years, until Columbus's time. The emir of Kuwait is planning to start an Arab settlement there with a mosque and an Islamic university.

The largest mosque in *Switzerland* is being built in Geneva, a Swiss newspaper article reported in 1978.

> "This building will be numbered among the treasures of contemporary art in this U.N. city," wrote the Geneva newspaper *La Suisse*. "It will become one of the sites of the city like the Cathedral of St. Peter." For the dedication at the end of May many prominent figures of the Islamic world were expected. King Khaled of Saudi Arabia, the founder and financier, is expected, or at least his prime minister. The land of Islam's origins is sending a reflection of its oriental magic to the City of the Nations. The mosque cost 11 million Swiss francs, and was to be completed in two years.[7]

This mosque is being built in one of the citadels of Swiss Protestantism, and yet neither the people nor the authorities seem to be aware of what is really involved. The Muslim world has a duty to subjugate the rest of the world, and mosques in Rome and Geneva are an important step in that process. The newspaper *Züri Leu* reported on November 11, 1977,

The mosque in Geneva. Hardly anyone is aware of what the construction of mosques in Rome, the citadel of Catholicism, or in Geneva, the citadel of Protestantism, means to the Muslim world.

"There are nearly 40 conversions [to Islam] every couple of weeks in Zurich. Their steadfastness is prayed for continually."

In *Belgium,* Islam is already officially recognized as a religious denomination. The state has taken on the payment of the *imam* (the cantor in the mosque), and the provincial governments will provide for the maintenance of the mosques. There are twenty mosques and around one hundred thousand Muslims in Belgium.

England is the site of the largest mosque in Western Europe. It is situated in Regent's Park, London, along with an Islamic university. At the international Islamic conference in London in 1976, it was said, "If we can win London for Islam, it won't be hard to win the whole Western world."

In 1945 there was one mosque in England, in 1950 there were twenty-five, in 1960 there were eighty, and in 1976 there were two hundred. Every sixth person in the world is already a Moslem. The Islamic view is that Christianity is a dying religion. London is supposed to serve as a strategic center in the West for the propagation of Islamic doctrine.

In *Austria*, the great victory by the Christian armies at the gates of Vienna over the Muslims nearly three hundred years ago has been turned into a defeat for the West. In 1683 the Vizier Cara Mustapha Pasha was slain in this battle, and his hopes of conquering the West were dashed. But now it would seem that victory is imminent, but not by the sword. A mosque, the first in Austria, is being erected in Vienna in a park on the Danube. King Khaled of Saudi Arabia is providing $3.25 million for the construction.

Into the Vacuum

Today Christians are spiritually weak. This paves the way for the triumphant march of Islam. In this ideological war, our front lines have been smashed through and overrun, the enemy is with us, and no one really recognizes it for what it is.

In 1979, more than one thousand Muslims met in a theater in Frankfurt, *Germany*, to demand that Islam be recognized as an official religion of Germany. *Die Welt* reported:

The mosque in Frankfurt. There are now one and one-half million Muslims in West Germany. During the first large gathering sponsored by the Islamic Cultural Center in April of 1979, Islamic chairman Demirgülle complained that Muslims in Germany were being given a hard time. He demanded the recognition of Islam as an official religion. A motion to this effect was made to the North Rhine-Westphalian Ministry of Culture.

Over the showcase with scenes from Brecht's "St. Joan of the Stockyards," the Turkish flag had been raised. The red flag with half moon and star was flapping in front of Frankfurt's Theater am Turm. Turkish imams were on the stage inside on this Easter Sunday, demanding recognition of Islam as an official religion.

About 1000 representatives from 158 Muslim congregations in West Germany had followed the call of the "Islamic Cultural Center" in Cologne to this first large Islamic conference. Frankfurt police cars patrolled continually past the theater and Turkish guards were posted at the entrance, to be prepared for possible disruptions by other Turkish groups. The "Islamic Cultural Center" considers itself an exclusively religious organization in contrast to the radical left groups and the radical right "Grey Wolves," which are politically oriented.

The president of the Islamic Center, Necdet Demirgülle, complained that Muslims in Germany were suffering a bad press in the media. Specifically, he said that Muslim parents are concerned about the religious instruction of their children. They fear the children could have their faith weakened and their cultural and national identity could be lost. It is the responsibility of the Muslim parents to give their children religious instruction from the Koran. This is difficult with the conflicting values taught them in German schools.

This can not change until Islam is recognized as an official religion in Germany. A motion to this effect has been made to the North Rhine-Westphalian Ministry of Culture. The spiritual leader of the Islamic Center, Harun Resit Tüyloglu, asked why the Federal Republic could not follow Belgium's example of recognizing Islam as an official religion. There are 1½ million Muslims in the Federal Republic, among them 1.2 million Turks. There are Koran schools for about 10,000 6- to 15-year-olds.

Demirgülle took issue with statements by Karl-Heinz Goebel, an official of the Department for Foreign Workers in the German League of Unions; the latter had claimed that the Koran schools incited the pupils to "reactionary fanaticism and enmity toward all other groups."

Islam, according to Demirgülle, harbors no aggressive intentions toward other religious or cultural groups: "In our Koran schools the thought is impressed on our pupils that they must be involved in the formation of our society and must live peaceably with one another. They should not forget that their parents came here to earn a living and that German-Turkish friendship has a long tradition.[8]

The Future of the Lie

For the mystery of lawlessness is already at work; only He who now restrains will do so until He is taken out of the way. And then the lawless one will be revealed, whom the Lord will consume with the breath of His mouth and destroy with the brightness of His coming. The coming of the lawless one is according to the working of Satan with all power, signs, and lying wonders, and with all deception of unrighteousness in those who perish, because they did not receive the love of the truth, that they might be saved. And for this reason God will send them strong delusion, that they should believe the lie, that they all might be condemned who did not believe the truth but had pleasure in unrighteousness (2 Thess. 2:7–12).

In the end times, lies will be believed because the love of the truth, that is the Bible, will diminish. Today there is only a crippled gospel in the world from which many have already turned away. Christians no longer seem to want to make the necessary commitment to change this situation. For instance, would we be willing to renounce our high standard of living for the sake of the truth? For most of us the answer is no.

I'm reminded of an Arab law officer who had just completed his studies in Europe. He visited us in Africa and stayed for the day. Before a meal I gave thanks. That evening he said, "That's the first time I ever heard a white man pray." Yet he had spent four years in a so-called Christian country.

But while Christians are becoming increasingly unconcerned, Islam has a goal of world domination. Ayatollah Khomeini has said, "If Islam were to really come into its own, all of mankind would be converted and all opposing ideologies would fall."

Islam's influence on the people in a country is complete. It governs their politics and way of living as well as their spiritual life. Its power can withstand any infiltration, whether of a material or spiritual nature. Qaddafi says, "The Koran is more modern than the revelations of the Jews or the Christians. Mohammed understood more about true socialism than Karl Marx." In the name of Islam, old laws and decrees are being put into practice.

> Thieves have their hand cut off, alcohol is not permitted, no man may practice the profession of hairdresser since no Muslim believer is al-

> lowed to touch a woman who is not his wife, no
> woman may drive a car. . . . The prophet refused
> to allow women free movement outside the walls
> of their houses.[9]

Our materialistic and spiritless Western world, grown insecure, can certainly not change the course Islam is going. And Islam can have no respect for a Christianity which is ashamed of itself, pretending to be alive while being dead.

One could apply to Christianity what the Ayatollah said of Islam: "If Christianity were to really come into its own, all of mankind would be converted and all opposing ideologies would fall." Unfortunately, our faith is even being denied by those who call themselves Christians.

At one time Europe had the highest literacy rate in history. Nearly everyone could have read the Bible. But we have ignored God's Word. There is a coming judgment for which we are not prepared. How long will it be until the dark storm clouds burst over the world? Islam suppresses the truth and puts lies in its place.

Dialogue or Monologue?

There is an appalling trend on the part of many Christians to treat Islam as an alternative way to God, completely denying the uniqueness of Christianity. A Vatican document, for instance, gives "Guidelines for a Dialogue between Christians and Muslims." In it Christians are advised to rethink their prejudices and their conception of Islam; they should realize how unjustly the Muslims have been treated by the West. The author claims that Allah is none other than the God of Moses and the God and Father of Jesus Christ!

Another document from the Second Vatican Council (1962-1965) with the title *Lumen Gentium* explains:

> The Muslims believe like Abraham; they pray with us to the one and only merciful God who will one day judge the world. The Muslims themselves have said they are against the habit of the Europeans of calling the Muslim God Allah, since they worship the same God.
>
> In the interest of furthering contact between the Church and Islam, the president of the Vatican Secretariat for non-Christians paid King Faisal of Saudi Arabia a visit. Pope Paul VI received the leading ulemas of Arabia in 1974. Msgr. Elchinger of Strasbourg received them in his cathedral and even invited them to say their prayers in front of the altar. They did it, bowing toward Mecca![10]

There is nothing wrong with talking with Muslims if it helps us understand them better, but why doesn't such dialogue cover such topics as the authenticity of Holy Scripture where there is a strong disagreement?

The strong has always enforced its will on the weak, and it would be a mistake to believe that this will change in relationships between Islam and Christianity. Islam believes it received Allah's highest and last revelation and that it is therefore the culmination of all religions. The Muslims believe they are the chosen people. The only reasonable relationship, in

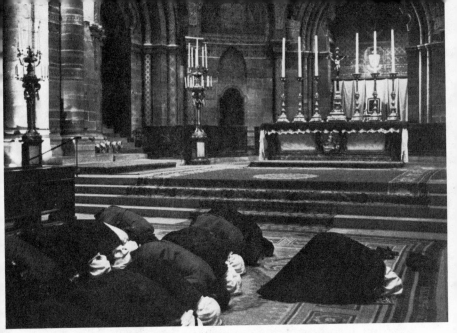

The Ulemas at prayer in the Strasbourg church.

the Muslim view, is for Christians and Jews to submit to Islam.

> O Believers! take not the Jews or Christians as friends. They are but one another's friends. If any one of you taketh them for his friends, he surely is one of them! God will not guide the evil doers (sura 5:56).

"Dialogue" to a Muslim can only mean what is expressed in the Koran.

> They say, moreover, "Become Jews or Christians that ye may have the *true* guidance." SAY: Nay! the religion of Abraham, the sound in faith, and not one of those who join gods with God (sura 2:129)!

And yet we are demonstrating again and again our lack of commitment to Christ by not defending our beliefs. We try to minimize the differences between us, and in so doing we are opening the way for Islamic domination. In 1976, there was a Christian-Islamic Colloquium in Tripoli, Libya. This report was filed.

> The Vatican sent a 14-man delegation with Cardinal Pignedoli as its head, president of the secretariat for non-Christians. The joint communique characterized Zionism as a doctrine which is "racist, aggressive, and foreign to Palestine and the Middle East." The text demanded the evacuation of all occupied territories and the recognition of the national rights of the Palestinian people, including their return to their native land.

> Regarding Jerusalem, the communique proclaimed the Arab character of the city, rejected its internationalization, and took issue with its Jewish character. (Neither the U.N., UNESCO, nor the Soviet Union had ever gone this far.)

> The goal of the meetings was to prepare a better world for the 1½ billion Christians and Moslems on earth. . . . After five days of hard discussion in a charged atmosphere, the Muslims reproached the Christians bitterly. Then Father Lanfry-Gross arose and publicly asked the Muslims for forgiveness for the accusations directed by Christians at the prophet Mohammed in the past. There was tumultuous applause. The sheiks cried, "Allah Akbar!" The Indian repre-

sentative said, "I felt the spirit of Allah hovering over the meeting."

No one would have expected at the beginning that the Vatican's representative would accept the most extreme Arab theses.

It is very important to note that the communique of Tripoli *was signed*. Thus the Vatican has allied itself with Arab extremists who want the destruction of Israel at whatever cost.[11]

This communique was later revoked by the Vatican, but the Muslim world looks only at the signature that is on the original document.

Just how far the fraternization between Christians and Moslems has progressed is seen in the following report in a Catholic weekly entitled "Friendly Meeting with the Muslims in Damascus."

On his week-long Eastern trip, Cardinal Koenig of Vienna met with Muslims in Damascus in an open and friendly discussion. He talked five times with the Grand Mufti of Syria, Sheik Keftaro. The Cardinal was invited into the mosque. There the Sheik spoke about Jesus and Mary in the Koran, with all the pastors of Damascus present, as well as the Orthodox Patriarch Yacoub. Then Cardinal Koenig referred to the common task of Christians and Muslims, monotheists all, of winning unbelievers back to the faith. To the applause of all present, the Sheik and the Cardinal embraced. Members of the Viennese foundation *Pro Oriente* pointed to this gesture as a sign of the good understanding between Muslims and Christians. This meeting, they say, takes on special importance in view of the civil war in Lebanon, which is still referred to erroneously as a religious war. Cardinal Koenig, who received a copy of the Koran as a gift from the Sheik, invited him to Vienna. [12]

Christians—especially Roman Catholics—are minimizing the differences between themselves and Muslims. In so doing they are betraying what they say they believe. Yet Islam takes itself very seriously. For instance, Saudi Arabia forbids all international airlines to fly over Mecca, the holy city. No unbeliever is permitted to see the holy place even from a plane. Where is there a Christian holy place that is revered in such a manner?

The largest mosque in Western Europe in London. During the International Islamic Conference in 1976, it was prophesied: "If we win London for Islam, it won't be hard to win the whole Western world."

In the "Dar-al-Islam," the land surrounding Mecca, everything without any connection to Islam is considered a "foreign body." Unbelievers would only contaminate this holy ground, and many an outsider has paid with his life for his ignorance of this, since Muslim law clearly states that the penalty for trespassing is death. The pope may invite as many ulemas to Rome as he desires; he would never be permitted to enter Mecca.

By chasing after the elusive goal of "brotherhood" with the Muslims, the Christian world is sealing its doom. A Christian church which has forsaken its foundation, Jesus Christ, no longer has a message for the world. It is no longer credible, viable, or prophetic.

5

Israel

Many people do not understand the historical relationship between Isaac and Ishmael. Not even Abraham was able to see the granting of his request: " 'Oh that Ishmael might live before Thee!' " (Gen. 17:18). Today Ishmael lives, but not before God! There are now 130 million Arabs in the Middle East; the angel's promise to Hagar has been fulfilled: " 'I will greatly multiply your descendants so that they shall be too many to count' " (Gen. 16:10).

God promised that He would make Abraham's descendants as numerous as the sands of the seashore through a son born to Sarah. But Abraham tried to bring about the fulfillment of God's promise by having a son by Sarah's handmaid Hagar.

> Now Sarah saw the son of Hagar the Egyptian, whom she had borne to Abraham, mocking. Therefore she said to Abraham, "Drive out this maid and her son, for the son of this maid shall not be an heir with my son" (Gen. 21:9,10).

The consequences of Abraham's acting according to the flesh are obvious today as we see the animosity between the children of Isaac and the children of Ishmael. God will not prevent us from acting in our own way rather than His, but we cannot hold the Lord responsible for the consequences.

Ishmael became an "anti-Isaac," a son of the flesh rather than of the promise. Twelve tribes proceeded from Ishmael, a reflection of Israel's blessing (see Gen. 17:20). Satan exploited this blessing and twenty-five hundred years later Islam was born. Today Ishmael's line is claiming the Promised Land, the promised blessing, that belongs to Isaac's children. The character of Ishmael has not changed to this day.

> And he will be a wild donkey of a man,
> His hand will be against everyone,
> And everyone's hand will be against him;
> And he will live to the east of all his brothers
> (Gen. 16:12).

The Mystery of Israel

"For I do not desire, brethren, that you should be ignorant of this mystery . . ." said the apostle Paul (Rom. 11:25). Paul mentioned three mysteries in his epistles: the mystery of Israel (see Rom. 9,10,11), the mystery of Christ and His church (see Eph. 5:32 and Col. 1:26,27), and the mystery of lawlessness (see 2 Thess. 2:7). The mystery of Israel is discussed in three chapters of Paul's epistle to the Romans. We have already examined Islam and the descendants of Ishmael. Now we turn our attention to the descendants of Isaac—the Jews.

Some Bible students spiritualize biblical prophecy about Israel, claiming that it does not refer to the actual

110

"Now Sarah saw the son of Hagar . . . mocking" (Gen. 21:9).

land of Israel or to the Jews. But when God says
through the prophets Moses, Ezekiel, Daniel, Paul,
and others that it is His purpose to gather the people of
Israel from the four corners of the earth and bring

them back to the land He gave their fathers, He means the physical land of Israel, not heaven or something else. When Paul speaks of the olive tree, he does not mean the church (sometimes referred to as a "spiritual Israel"), but to the real Israel from whom salvation comes.

Throughout all history Israel has been the minute hand on God's clock, and this is true today also. Spiritualizing biblical prophecy about Israel to make it refer to the church does not fit the facts. We must take the promises to Israel literally.

Throughout the Old and New Testaments it was prophesied that Israel would be scattered throughout the earth and then brought together again. The formation of the state of Israel is a sign of the imminent return of the Messiah.

> "Lift up your eyes and look around;
> All of them gather together, they come to you
> . . ." (Is. 49:18).

> ". . . in the latter years you will come into the land that is restored from the sword, whose inhabitants have been gathered from many nations to the mountains of Israel which had been a continual waste . . ." (Ezek. 38:8).

> ". . . in that day . . . I will make Jerusalem a heavy stone for all the peoples . . ." (Zech. 12:3).

The nations surrounding Israel, as well as the superpowers, will continue their armament for the final battle.

> For they are the spirits of demons, working signs, which go out to the kings of the earth and of the whole world, to gather them to the battle of that great day of God Almighty (Rev. 16:14).

It is worth noting that immediately following this statement, the return of the Messiah is announced: " 'Behold, I am coming as a thief. Blessed is he who watches, and keeps his garments, lest he walk naked and they see his shame' " (v. 15).

At the time of Christ's first coming the "times of the Gentiles," or the church age, began, and Israel was set aside for a time as the instrument of God's activity in the world. But neither Paul nor Jesus ever tried to abolish the Law (the Torah) as the Pharisees claimed. Paul made it very clear that Israel would not be rejected finally (see Rom. 11:1). He never put the church in Israel's place, nor vice-versa. Both have their time and their purpose. The fulfillment of the prophecy of Israel's regathering was postponed until the end times. At that point Israel was to be brought back to the center stage of world history.

For nearly two thousand years Israel has waited while the times of the Gentiles has run its course. In Romans 11:12 Paul explains that if the setting aside of Israel was a blessing to the heathen, its return will be a greater blessing throughout the world.

God Fulfills His Promise

Paul clearly believed that Israel would be restored. Ezekiel also prophesied that God had said,

> "And I will bring them out from the peoples and
> gather them from the countries and bring them
> to their own land; and I will feed them on the
> mountains of Israel, by the streams, and in all the
> inhabited places of the land" (Ezek. 34:13).

In addition, in Ezekiel 37 the prophet records a dramatic vision in which dead, dry bones come to life, an allusion to the restoration of Israel.

The end of the times of the Gentiles will come not when all heathen are converted, but in God's own time. Over the last two thousand years Christians have been anxiously looking for the restoration of Israel. Even before the Lord ascended into heaven, His disciples asked Him, " 'Lord, will You at this time restore the kingdom to Israel?' " (Acts 1:6).

Today it is easy to see that the restoration of Israel is a fulfillment of biblical prophecy, since today the state of Israel actually exists. Yet, Christians of earlier generations also saw clearly that, according to the Bible, the restoration of Israel would be an important sign that the end of the age was at hand. These people were waiting for the fulfillment of God's promises, not because they were prophets but simply because they believed the prophetic words of Scripture.

Jung Stilling (1740–1817) said,

> The true Christian has always looked to the
> golden clock hands on the temple turrets; who-
> ever had poor eyes asked those with sharper
> vision what time it was. . . . The conversion of
> this remarkable people and its return to its
> fatherland will open the eyes of many. . . . In the

eyes of the world, then, the Bible will be legitimized and we will all know where we stand.

In 1914, Vladimir Gelesnov said,

Israel remains Israel. The banished are to return to their homeland; their capital will be theirs again. They are to be a new, sacred, royal, priestly nation. If this seems a bit too unlikely, we should remember that it is God's statement that He will bring it to pass.

Because of events like the Dreyfus Affair, Theodor Herzl's Zionist activities, and the Third Reich's "Final Solution,"* preparations for modern Israel were made. We must pay attention to events that might have prophetic significance. Two thousand years ago God intervened in history with the first coming of His Son: " '. . . salvation is of the Jews' " (John 4:22). God is intervening in history again through Israel to pre-

---

*Alfred Dreyfus, a Jew, was a French general staff officer unfairly accused of treason in 1894 and banished to Devil's Island for life. The French army was permeated by anti-Semitism at that time. The affair became a political issue, and eventually the case was reopened and Dreyfus's sentence was reduced to ten years. Finally, however, in 1906 Dreyfus was exonerated, reinstated as a major, and decorated with the Legion of Honor. The Dreyfus Affair helped to unite the political left wing and bring it to power in France. Theodor Herzl organized the first World Zionist Congress in 1897 and was a leader in the movement for the formation of a Jewish nation state. Hitler's "Final Solution" was a governmental directive that had as its goal the extermination of all Jews and other so-called misfits. (Editor).

pare for the Second Coming of the Messiah. There are no puzzle pieces missing in the political, military, or prophetic realm. Everything is ready.

Israel: God's Touchstone for the World

We should be aware that Israel is God's touchstone for the world, used to test the purity and genuineness of other nations' love for God. God did not choose Israel because of any quality in it, but for His own name's sake. The real issue at hand is not Israel, but God's plans. God is using Israel to work out His own plan for the world. Nations will be judged on their attitude toward Israel. But one by one they will give up on Israel because of the importance of oil for their economies. Make no mistake about it: When the prophecies concerning Israel are fulfilled, those concerning the rest of the world will also be fulfilled. Israel's return to its own land has made the affairs of all nations interdependent. God has said,

> "And the LORD your God will inflict all these curses on your enemies, and on those who hate you, who persecuted you" (Deut. 30:7).

> . . . and those who harass Judah will be cut off . . . (Is. 11:13).

> For thus says the LORD of hosts, "After glory He has sent me against the nations which plunder you, for he who touches you touches the apple of His eye" (Zech. 2:8).

We are not witnessing merely a battle between two

national groups, but a battle between the God of heaven and the "prince of the power of the air, the spirit who now works in the sons of disobedience" (Eph. 2:2).

The whole world is being drawn into the Middle Eastern conflict. We are now either instruments for the perfection of the saints through the inspired Word of God, or instruments of coming chaos through unbelief. God has prophesied a battle in which He will destroy His enemies.

> "And My holy name I shall make known in the midst of My people Israel; and I shall not let My holy name be profaned any more. And the nations will know that I am the Lord, the Holy One in Israel.
> "Behold, it is coming and it shall be done, declares the Lord God. That is the day of which I have spoken" (Ezek. 39:7,8).

This battle will lead to the destruction of the nations allied against Israel. They will be deceived into thinking their security lies with Ishmael. When the Israelites fled Egypt, they were in great danger but were saved by the Red Sea miracle. The Israelites are again finding themselves in great danger but will again be saved by a miracle of God. We are seeing the prelude to the last attempt by Satan to destroy God's chosen people here on earth.

Jesus knew that the times of the Gentiles would come to an end when Jerusalem belonged to Israel again. " '. . . Jerusalem will be trampled by the Gentiles until the times of the Gentiles are fulfilled,' " He said (Luke 21:24). At that time the city will be beseiged by an army whose goal is the annihilation of Jerusalem. This army will be pitted in a holy war—a *jihad*—against Israel. Jesus said, " 'And when you see Jerusalem surrounded by armies, then know that its desolation is near' " (Luke 21:20). Jerusalem will be an offense to the whole world. The nations will forsake her and even support the army surrounding her. " 'Therefore when you see the "abomination of desolation," spoken of by Daniel the prophet, standing in the holy place' (whoever reads, let him understand) . . ." (Matt. 24:15).

At the holy place in Jerusalem an anti-Christian, anti-Messianic, anti-Israel religious power will be located. This is why Jesus never speaks of the temple when referring to this time but of the "abomination of desolation" in Jerusalem.

If God were not to intervene in this conflict, it would lead to the world's destruction. Human life would not be possible. But He will intervene.

> "And then the sign of the Son of Man will appear in heaven, and then all the tribes of the earth will mourn, and they will see the Son of Man coming on the clouds of heaven with power and great glory" (Matt. 24:30).

The Son of Man is Jesus Christ. His return was prophesied by two angels at the time he ascended into heaven.

> "This same Jesus, who was taken up from you into heaven, will so come in like manner as you have seen Him go into heaven" (Acts 1:11).

According to Zechariah, the Lord will then

> go forth and fight against those nations, . . . and in that day His feet will stand on the Mount of Olives, which is in front of Jerusalem on the east . . . (Zech. 14:3,4).

Israel Throughout History

Throughout history Israel has suffered at the hands of other nations—the Persians, the Babylonians, the Egyptians, the Romans. Jesus had been dead only about forty years when Titus led his vengeful legions into Jerusalem. Hunger, pestilence, and the sword claimed their victims. One million Jews died during the seige of the city in A.D. 70.

The following centuries brought more troubles to the children of Israel. They were despised, rejected, and at the mercy of persecutors, as the Lord had said. " 'And among these nations you shall find no rest, and there shall be no resting place for the sole of your foot; but there the LORD will give you a trembling heart . . .' " (Deut. 28:65).

In the Middle Ages the Crusaders assaulted every Jew they met on their way to Palestine. "Let them be slaughtered and the name of Israel banished forever from the earth!" they cried. The blood of Abraham's sons flowed in streams throughout the world. Let me give you one example.

In Mainz, Germany, the palace of the Archbishop Rothardus was being stormed by fanatics. Seven hundred Jews thought they had found refuge there, but they were wrong: Men, women, and children were slain by the sword. Those who escaped to their homes killed themselves to avoid the Crusaders' swords. Mothers even killed the child at their breast! Everywhere prisons were filled with Jews. They were sold, plundered, disenfranchised. They were accused of practicing magic and sacrificing children, and they were banished from various countries. Their throats were cut, or they were hanged between two dogs.

In the fourteenth century a terrible pestilence called the Black Death broke out in Europe and quickly killed one third of the people. "The Jews have poisoned the wells!" "Kill the sons of Israel!" those that remained cried. More than one million Jews died. Truly their history is one of blood and tears.

From the beginning of the Reformation, the Protestant world has not been kind to the Jews. The consequences of this have yet to be overcome in the church and in the world.

As a young man Luther was friendly to Jews. In the hour of his greatest need he was visited by two Jews at the Diet of Worms. In 1523 he even fought against those who hated Jews. He wrote:

> Popes, bishops, sophists, monks, and other fools treated Jews like dogs. They were called names and had their belongings stolen. Yet they are blood-brothers and cousins of the Savior. No other people has been singled out by God as they have; they have been entrusted with His holy Word.[1]

Since Luther was convinced he was living in the end times, he concluded that the Jews had to be converted.

But when that did not happen as he thought it should, Luther changed his attitude toward them.

> The Jews deserve the most severe penalties. Their synagogues should be leveled, their homes destroyed, they should be exiled into tents like the gypsies. [It is noteworthy that the gypsies were included in the Nazis' "final solution."] Their religious writings should be taken from them. The rabbis should be forbidden to continue teaching the Law. All professions should be closed to them. Only the hardest, coarsest work should be permitted them. Rich Jews should have their fortunes confiscated, and the money used to support Jews who are willing to be converted. If all these measures are unsuccessful, the Christian princes have the duty of driving the Jews from their lands as they would rabid dogs.[2]

Luther praised King Ferdinand, even though he was a Catholic, for driving Jews from Spain. Luther even called them devils: "It is as difficult to convert a Jew as it is to convert the devil. He has a heart of iron like the devil. They are children of the devil, condemned to the flames of hell."[3]

Four days before his death, February 18, 1546, Luther preached his last sermon. The subject matter was the Jews. He demanded that they be driven from all German lands.

This same kind of thinking has appeared in the church throughout history. Too often the Jew is treated with hatred rather than sympathy.

> The Christian must battle fanatically against the Jews, for they are the arch enemies of Christianity and the human race. They are condemned to eternal slavery since they crucified the Lord.

> The eight sermons of Johannes Chrysostomus in 387 A.D. against the Jews in Antioch are of epochal importance. Gathered together here is the whole arsenal of weapons against the Jews: the Jew is lecherous, slippery, fleshly; a murderer of the prophets and of Jesus. He honors the devil. He is a criminal, a drunkard, a whoremaster. He is the "murderer of God."

> Hieronymus gave a much-quoted, much referred to tirade against the synagogue: it is a brothel, a den of iniquity, the home of the devil, a gaping abyss. No matter what it is called, it deserves worse.[4]

Even to the present day, Rome has not recognized the state of Israel. If it did, it would have to admit that saints, bishops, and popes have erred in their evaluations and attitudes towards the Jews.

The Church's Mistake

The more the church denies the significance of the Jews and their unique place in the plan of God, the more its witness becomes unfruitful and questionable. It is wrong, for instance, to assume that the church has taken Israel's place. God is faithful, and He does not regret His bond with Israel. God has made only two convenants: one with Israel on Sinai and the other with the church by the sacrifice of His Son on the cross (see Matt. 26:28). God's faithfulness will see that the covenants are honored. Although a relationship with God today can only be built upon the terms of the covenant with the church—". . . for there is no other name under heaven [besides Jesus'] given among men by which we must be saved" (Acts 4:12)—God still has a very special relationship with the Jews which will be renewed in the last days.

When we set the church against the Jews, we are trying to set one covenant against another. The real issue, however, is how we react to the Covenant Maker Himself. We need to listen to Pastor Duvernoy.

Christ as well as His servant Saul of Tarsus, the Church's principal theologian, bind the fate of the Christian community to that of Israel. Thus Jewish history must remain central in the mind of the Church and remain the cornerstone of its theology. Born in Israel, raised in the milieu of the Temple and developed in the synagogues of the Roman Empire, the Church goes side by side with the synagogue through the centuries.

The theology of the Church is mainly one of grace. If it ceases to be anchored in the rock of this grace, it becomes instead a cold institution and a system of dogma which has led in the past to religious wars and the Inquisition. Since the apostolic era this institution has proclaimed not a theology of grace but a rigid dogma of contempt for its Jewish mother. The fruits of this have been burnings of heretics, gold stars, ghettos and pogroms.

Instead of teaching that Christ's death was also for Israel, the Church has taught for centuries that the Jews killed Jesus. Instead of teaching that His blood brings forgiveness to the synagogue also, it has excluded the Jews from His salvation—in the name of that very blood! Instead of teaching with Paul that God always grants His people the blessings He has promised, it has taught that God has rejected His chosen people. Instead of love, it has taught hate.

Through the coarse, merciless, final judgments of the church fathers, Luther, and numerous theologians, the Church unwittingly paved the way for the Nazi persecutions.

Now, at the time of the restoration of the land and its capital, Jerusalem, the Church refuses to see the hand of God in it and to recognize the capital (the only capital in the world which bears God's name!). This could only happen if the Church forgot that the Jewish nation remains in the center of God's grace. . . .

The church is confused by the re-awakening of Zion; it is angered by talk of "Zionist theology." How ironic! It is its own theology, that of Christ and Paul. What is this theology based on? The eternal faithfulness of God and the promises given to the fathers, the prophets, King David, and the apostles.[5]

Israel Today

To this day the blood of Christ hangs over the Jews like a curse. Let us pray that this precious blood will soon become a blessing to them, for they are after all brothers of Jesus after the flesh. It is not our task to avenge the injustice done to Jesus. Let us rather hold our tongues and humble ourselves because of our own misdeeds. We should remember that in spite of all their errors and sufferings, the Jews are God's people. If we bless where our forefathers cursed and if we take in those who are cast out, we will escape the judgment which is coming on the persecutors of Israel.

Although Israel is stronger today politically than it has been in more than two thousand years, she has not changed in religious and intellectual terms. To be convinced of this, one must go into a synagogue. Instead of a Levitical ritual, there is a gathering of brokers coming and going during the public prayers, children playing, people whose attitude betrays apathy if not contempt, rabbis who repeat the old prayer formulas in an indifferent manner—praises and supplications foreign to the heart and conscience.

Today Jewish children study traditions, or rather miserable old legends, of their forefathers or vain laws of their Talmud teachers, or spiritually damaging writings of modern infidels. They do not possess the Word of God, except perhaps excerpts from it. They are taken up with material interests. These occurrences appear to be a fulfillment of Romans 11:10: "Let their eyes be darkened that they may not see,/And bow down their back always." A most lamentable ignorance has them in its grip. The *tallith* is the cloth with which they cover their heads during the reading of the Law, an unwitting symbol of a "veil" that seems to be before their eyes when the books of Moses are read.

Israel today has practically nothing: The kingly rule has been given over to the heathen (see Daniel 2 and 7); the priesthood, the prophecy, even the knowledge of Scriptures belongs to the *goyim* (Gentiles). False worldly wisdom is seducing some Jews, superstition is taking its toll of others. Without Jesus Christ, without God, without hope, the Jew is as Isaiah describes him: restless and a fugitive on the earth. If he gazes upward: darkness! If he looks down: more darkness!

> And they will pass through the land hard-pressed and famished, and it will turn out that when they are hungry, they will be enraged and curse their king and their God as they face upward (Is. 8:21).

On the one hand Jews know from the Law that a sacrifice is necessary for the forgiveness of sins; on the other hand they are faced with the impossibility of offering a sacrifice since the Law permits none outside the temple in Jerusalem. What terrible straits will their conscience be in when it awakens!

The time has not yet come when all of Israel can be reached with the gospel. Our labors are insufficient; the conversion of the Jewish nation is a miracle that Jesus Christ has reserved for Himself. Yet with God's help, the work of Christians will contribute to the salvation of some.

Israel also deserves our attention because of the

glorious promises God has given it. He has promised its restoration and renewed influence throughout the world. By any stretch of the imagination, the Jewish nation should have given up completely in the course of the last few centuries. But God, true to His promises, has preserved it in marvelous fashion. Israel in its affliction is much like the burning bush at Horeb that could not be consumed. Dispersed like no other people, oppressed from all sides, it has remained true to its principles and doctrines with such stamina that one could search in vain for a parallel in world history. It has stubbornly held to a form of religion, almost without feeling. The Jews have in their services the same language, the same Scriptures, the same rites and customs as they did millenia ago.

Many former blossoming nations have disappeared. One writer said:

> The names of other nations are all that is left; they have passed on like drops of water in the ocean. On the other hand, the Jews, entering this great ocean [of history], did not become dissolved in the waves, but sank to the bottom to be preserved like precious stones.

> The fact that this people, always distinguishable from surrounding peoples, retained its national identity must be acknowledged as an irrefutable proof of divine prophecy (Amos 9:8 ff.).

> Another proof is that God has kept Israel for so long and in such a miraculous way in spite of so many possibilities of destruction, simply to gather her again by His great and eternal mercy.

Should the God of Abraham, who has proven Himself so true and honest in His chastisements, not be just the same in His blessing? The hour is near when the Shepherd of Israel will gather the wandering sheep of His pasture from out of the whole world. That will be the starting point for a new period of world history. The restoration of His people and the conversion of the world through them is according to prophecy the goal that God has continually before His eyes.

To most of us, the Russians, the Germans, the Turks, or the French with their confusing and conflicting interests are often unsettling. But to the Lord, the Jews are the focus of events in our world and the eventual source of its happiness. The changeable events on the world stage should be seen in this light. Soon Daniel's seventieth "week of years" which had been postponed will begin and the long interval of the "times of the Gentiles" will come to its end. Jerusalem will be liberated.[6]

The Choice

The state of Israel is no accident. It is the re-creation of a nation foretold by God and brought into being in God's time. Israel is the object of God's unending love. He calls it His "dear son" (using the term "Ephraim") in Jeremiah 31:20—right at the time He was about to judge it severely. If God loves this people so much, how can Christians be led astray to hate them?

Christianity has a heritage rooted in Judaism—not in Islam nor the Koran. There is no common destiny between Judaism and Islam. If the Koran is true, then

Christianity and Judaism will one day dissolve. But if the Bible is true, then events will make a place for Israel in the end times.

To reject Israel is to reject our own background. It is to reject the tree into which we have been grafted if we are Christians. It is a continual grief to me that Christians are not aware of this fact—a result of not knowing the Bible.

God's ways were revealed and entrusted to Israel, who has passed this knowledge on to us. From Israel came the prophets and apostles. From Israel came the Messiah. To Israel belong Paul, Silas, Peter, and all the courageous messengers of the Lord. These Jewish Christians braved many dangers, deprivations, and sacrifices to transmit the message of the love of God to our forefathers, who otherwise would have been in total darkness and without hope in the world.

The Jewish church fathers were all sons of Jacob and brothers of the Jew whom we meet from time to time, and perhaps despise. The world is turning its face once again from this most despised and unworthy son. But "remember that you do not support the root, but the root supports you" (Rom. 11:18).

> We proud people forget that so easily. If we have heard the prayer of Abraham for the heathen, if David's harp has ever given our restless soul peace, if ever the efforts of Paul, Peter, and John or especially the sufferings of our Savior have touched us, then we should have mercy on their brothers.[7]

Will we have the courage to repent, or will we make the wrong choice? We cannot blame our forefathers for

129

their unfortunate acts, since their vision was limited. But we have no excuse. We live in a time in which it becomes clearer each day (just read the newspaper!) that prophecy concerning Israel is heading toward fulfillment.

The nations of the world accuse the Jews for not having assimilated into the countries in which they live, forgetting that the host countries gave them no opportunity to do so. Rejection and persecution hardly speed up assimilation. This persecution, of course, was all under the pretense that the Jews were the murderers of Jesus. The children of Israel have become "wandering Jews" through no choice of their own, and until quite recently they did not even have a homeland.

If the nations do not bring God and His Word into the conferences and deliberations, nor change course with respect to Israel, they will be to blame for the coming world conflict.

The time is coming when the Spirit of God will be restrained and will no longer convict the world of sin through the inspired Word. The end and judgment cannot be far away.

The whole earth has been brought into dependence on the False Prophet. In the battle of the Middle East the Christian world will have to make a choice for Jesus Christ or for the False Prophet.

The awakening giant of Islam rubs its eyes and realizes with amazement that suddenly everything is falling into its lap and that it possesses everything necessary to bring the whole world under its influence. The Koran predicted a time when Muslims would dominate the world, and now it seems to them that the moment for the fulfillment of Allah's promise has come. The Muslims know there must be no time nor energy lost in carrying out the necessary program. Since their system is a religious one, world domination will be religious as well as political and economic.

Jews . . . Muslims . . . Christians

Both the Jews and Arabs claim that Abraham is their father. And, in fact, he was the father of both Isaac and Ishmael. When Jesus spoke to some Jews about freedom, for instance, they replied, " 'We are Abraham's descendants, and were never in bondage to anyone' " (John 8:33). The Koran, however, says, "Abraham was neither Jew nor Christian; but he was sound in the faith, a Muslim; and not of those who add gods to God" (3:60).

A very important question, therefore, is whether the God of Abraham is the god the Arabs describe or the God the Jews perceive. But perhaps there is a third alternative. Christians believe that only when a person acknowledges and submits to the Bible, the Word of God, will he perceive who the true God is. Jesus Christ said, " 'If you continue in My word, then you are My disciples indeed. And you shall know the truth, and the truth shall make you free' " (John 8:31,32).

Both Jews and Muslims accept Abraham and reject Christ, and yet He told them the truth which He had heard directly from the Father.

> ". . . you seek to kill Me, a Man who has told you the truth which I have heard from God. Abraham did not do this. You do the deeds of your

131

father." Then they said to Him, "We were not born of fornication; we have one Father—God." Jesus said to them, "If God were your Father, you would love Me, for I proceeded forth and came from God; nor did I come of Myself, but He sent Me. Why do you not understand My speech? Because you are not able to listen to My word. You are of your father the devil, and the desires of your father you want to do. He was a murderer from the beginning, and does not stand in the truth, because there is no truth in him. When he speaks a lie, he speaks from his own resources, for he is a liar and the father of it" (John 8:40–44).

Jesus is the Anointed of God (the Messiah), the eternally existing One, the One who is and was and is to come. A person who claims to have Abraham as father and who wants to worship the God of Abraham should know that Jesus Christ is the only way to the God of Abraham. Jesus said, " 'Most assuredly, I say to you, he who does not enter the sheepfold by the door, but climbs up some other way, the same is a thief and a robber' " (John 10:1). Only in and through Christ—not through Allah, not through the ceremonies of the synagogue—can we be truly Abraham's children.

"He who has the Son [Jesus Christ] has life; he who does not have the Son of God does not have life" (1 John 5:12).

Belief in Fairy Tales

The speaker at a meeting of the National Association

of Arab Americans (with a membership of 1.5 million) said, "We wish the members in the Congress would stop believing fairy tales about the Middle East, such as the biblical right of the Jewish people to Palestine."

This points up one of the basic differences between Arabs and Christians. To the Muslim the Bible is not authoritative. All religious writings, except the Koran and some related writings, are fairy tales. To them, the Bible is not true.

But how many Christians have actually read the Bible? How many believe that it is the inspired Word of God in its entirety? How many believe that "All Scripture is given by inspiration of God, and is profitable for doctrine, for reproof, for correction, for instruction in righteousness" (2 Tim. 3:16)?

Make no mistake: Islam will not stop at the destruction of Israel. Anyone not submitting to it will be attacked and annihilated. Today this attitude shows through only once in a while, but it will become evident more and more often as the Islamic world becomes increasingly conscious of its power.

Forty-seven years have passed since Hitler took power in Germany. Once again, however, Israel is faced with destruction. Nearly the same methods are being put to use, yet the world is silent. The Young Muslim People's Front comments concerning Persian Jews: "Every generation needs its Hitler to weed out the Jewish vegetation. Leave our land or be slaughtered whether you are young or old."[8]

Such hatred and its effects will certainly not stop with Israel, but will draw the whole earth into a conflict. Since this rage is directed mainly against Jews and Christians, it is ultimately against God and His

Word. In his book *The Islamic Republic*, the Ayatollah Khomeini preaches resistance to the "conspiracy of Christians and Jews against Islam." Since the Koran calls the Muslims the chosen people (see sura 3:106ff.), any other people making this claim are blaspheming Allah.

The battle is between Allah and Jehovah. There are but two alternatives: "He who is not with Me is against Me, and He who does not gather with Me scatters" (Luke 11:23).

The Staging of the Last Act

The restoration of the nation of Israel is the signal announcing the end times. Israel is the catalyst for the unification of the Arab world. Any peace between Egypt or any other Arab nation and Israel can last only a short time, because peace would make the Arab unity more questionable. The prince of this world is sparing no effort or means to blind the eyes of the nations so that they will not recognize the signs of the times.

However, thirty-five hundred years ago, God said through Moses,

> "So it shall become when all of these things have come upon you, the blessing and the curse which I have set before you, and you call them to mind in all the nations where the LORD your God has banished you, and you return to the LORD your God and obey Him with all your heart and soul according to all that I command you today, you and your sons, then the LORD your God will restore you from captivity, and have compassion

on you, and will gather you again from all the peoples where the LORD your God has scattered you.

"If your outcasts are at the ends of the earth, from there the LORD your God will gather you, and from there He will bring you back.

"And the LORD your God will bring you unto the land which your fathers possessed, and you shall possess it; and He will prosper you and multiply you more than your fathers" (Deut. 30:1–5).

And then about twenty-seven hundred years ago God said through the prophet Isaiah:

Then it will happen on that day that the Lord
Will again recover the second time with His
  hand
The remnant of His people, who will remain,
From Assyria, Egypt, Pathros, Cush, Elam, Shi-
  nar, Hamath
And from the islands of the sea.
And He will lift up a standard for the nations,
And will assemble the banished ones of Israel,
And will gather the dispersed of Judah
From the four corners of the earth (Is. 11:11,12).

Although the immediate setting for this prophecy is the return of the Jews from the Babylonian captivity, it looks beyond that to the end times when the nation of Israel will be restored and God's chosen people will be gathered from throughout the world.

About twenty-six hundred years ago God said through the prophet Jeremiah:

> "But, 'As the Lord lives, who brought up the sons of Israel from the land of the north and from all the lands where He had banished them.' For I will restore them to their own land which I gave to their fathers" (Jer. 16:15).

At about the same time He said through Zephaniah:

> "At that time I will bring you in,
> Even at the time when I gather you together; for I will give you renown and praise
> Among all the peoples of the earth,
> When I restore your fortunes before your eyes,"
> says the LORD (Zeph. 3:20).

And through Zechariah:

> "I will whistle for them to gather them together,
> For I have redeemed them;
> And they will be as numerous as they were before.
> When I scatter them among the peoples,
> They will remember Me in far countries,
> And they with their children will live and come back" (Zech. 10:8,9).

A New Heaven and New Earth

Except for the last two thousand years, God's dealings with the world have been focused on the nation of Israel. However, the times of the Gentiles are about to end, and Israel will be central once more. The rejection of Israel by the United Nations marks the rift that is occurring between Israel and the other nations of the world. Since Israel's fate—and not that of the United States or its allies—is bound up with the fate of God's people, what happens in the Middle East is more important than what happens in the United States or England.

Indeed the human race could not have revealed its own downfall any more clearly than it already has. If God gives man self-determination, he is soon licentious (cf. the time before Noah); if God gives him authority, he is soon guilty of oppression (cf. the time after Noah); if God gives him a promise, he soon sinks into disbelief (cf. the time of the patriarchs and following); if God shows him that he has been unrighteous, he soon clothes himself in self-righteousness (cf. the time of the giving of the Law); if God gives him Christ the Savior, he soon chooses an antichrist (cf. the time of the gospels); if God gives him a king, he soon becomes rebellious (cf. the Millennium).

Thus mankind is continually in revolt against God. As Israel is on a small scale, so is mankind on a larger one: "a people who err in their heart" (Ps. 95:10). No wonder all historical periods end with a judgment of God:

- the Paradise in the Garden of Eden with the expulsion of Adam and Eve
- the antediluvian period with the Flood
- the post-Flood period with Babel
- the period of the Law with the destruction of the nation of Israel
- the church age with the anti-Christian tribulation

- the Millennium with annihilation and flames (see Rev. 20:9).

"But then, when all thinkable possibilities have been exhausted and the worldly kingdom has consumed itself, God's Kingdom will appear triumphantly (Rev. 11:15) with 'new heavens and a new earth, in which righteousness dwell' (2 Peter 3:13)."[9]

6

Jerusalem

The heart and spirit of Israel is Jerusalem. Through-out history battles have been fought and wars waged over what Jews, Christians, and Muslims alike call the Holy City. From the Old Testament battles of the Canaanites, to the destruction of the city by the Romans in A.D. 70, to the rule of the British in this century, Jerusalem has been the center of men's affections and fighting.

When the United Nations drew up guidelines for the partition of Palestine in 1947, Jerusalem was to have become an international city administered by a UN official. But instead Jerusalem became the scene of bloody fighting between Israeli and Arab forces which resulted in the Arabic country of Jordan holding the Old City and the Israelis holding the New City. Jerusalem became a divided city. But in the six-day war of 1967, Israel captured the Jordanian half and has administered it since then.

In May, 1979, an Arabic-Islamic conference in Morocco was held to discuss the liberation of Jerusalem. Reportedly a secret plan was set up whereby oil was to be used as a weapon and a means of pressure. Jerusalem, *al Quds* (the Holy City), must no longer remain in the hands of the unbelievers, it was said; it must be taken back at any cost! No sacrifice was too great. When the conference was dismissed, the delegates called to one another, "Until next year in Jerusalem!"

But in July, 1980, the Israeli parliament, the Knesset, declared all of Jerusalem to be the undivided and "eternal" capital of Israel. At least twelve Arab countries, led by Saudi Arabia and Iraq, immediately began putting pressure on those countries that had embassies in Jerusalem instead of Tel Aviv. Holland was told that if it didn't move its embassy out of Jerusalem within thirty days, all oil from Kuwait and Libya would be cut off. At the end of August the UN Security Council voted to call on UN members to move their embassies out of Jerusalem. Saudi Arabia's Crown Prince Fahd asked all Arab countries to unite in a *jihad* to liberate all of the Israeli-occupied territories claimed by the Arabs—especially the Old City of Jerusalem.

Zechariah could not have been more accurate when he said twenty-five hundred years ago that Jerusalem would be " 'a cup that causes reeling to all the peoples around' " (Zech. 12:2). Many people will try to solve the conflicts surrounding Jerusalem, but those involved will find that their involvement with Jerusalem will be the cause of their own downfall, for it will be " 'a heavy stone for all the peoples; all who lift it will be severely injured. And all the nations of the earth will be gathered against it' " (Zech. 12:3).

Jerusalem and Islam

Most of us in the West know the importance of

140

Jerusalem to both Jews and Christians. Yet Moslems also lay claim to Jerusalem with the spiritual authority of Islam, "the last and highest revelation of Allah." The basis of this claim is shown in a pamphlet published by the German Protestant Council on Missions.

Most Christians are surprised that Jerusalem means as much to the Mohammedans as it does to the Jews. When Muslims recite the first surah during their time of prayer, they are thinking, perhaps unconsciously, of Jerusalem. They know from the Koran that the original direction of prayer was toward Jerusalem, not Mecca.

In the middle of the first surah is a reminder of the day of judgment. According to an old tradition, God will hold final judgment at Jerusalem. Many devout Muslims see the fighting today in and around Palestine as the prelude to the world's final battles. This Palestinian conflict has turned the interest of the world toward Jerusalem. Millions of Arabs are singing the Jerusalem song of the Lebanese singer Fairus:

For thee, City of Prayer, I pray.
For thee, most brilliant of dwelling-places,
    thou blossom of cities.
O Jerusalem, thou City of Prayer . . .

In the last verse comes the warning of the end:

Radiant anger is coming.
With terrible steeds he is coming like the wind,
And the countenance of violence will fall slain.
The Temple belongs to us—Jerusalem is ours.

> With our hands we shall restore the splendor of
> Jerusalem.
> With our hands . . . to Jerusalem . . . Peace . . .
> Peace. . . .[1]

Muslims have strong feelings about Jerusalem because of their history. The site of the temple mentioned in the song is Mount Moriah in the center of Jerusalem, which has been for ages a memorial to Abraham, father of Arabs and Jews alike. Moriah is supposed to be the place where Abraham went to offer Isaac as a sacrifice. Even more importantly, it was here, according to sura 17 of the Koran, that Mohammed was taken directly to heaven at night.

Two of the oldest and most venerable Islamic edifices have been constructed on Mount Moriah: The Al Aqsa Mosque and the Dome of the Rock. To this day they dominate the skyline of Jerusalem. Muslim pilgrims have come here for centuries. Next to Mecca and Medina, Jerusalem is the holiest place in Islam. For the Arab its very name means "the holy place."

Jerusalem became part of the Islamic world quite early: In 638—only six years after the death of Mohammed—Caliph Omar took the city without bloodshed or destruction. It has belonged to the Islamic world ever since, with the exception of the time of the Crusades and the modern restoration of Israel.

Islamic mystics and theologians have left their influence here. Business and daily life in Jerusalem are typically Arabic; the majority of the population, before the restoration of the city to Israel, were Arabs. Muslims do not contest the fact that Christians (especially Arab Christians) and Jews also have close ties to this unique city. What they resent is that the city is now completely under Jewish control and is being "Israelized" single-mindedly. They want self-determination for the Moslem population. They want it to be an open city where adherents of three religions can coexist peaceably.

Islamic Commitment to the Holy City

Because Jerusalem means so much to Muslims, they do not want to see it under Israeli control.

> King Faisal, who felt himself to be the protector of all Muslim holy places, died in 1975. He continually referred to the fact that Jerusalem is precious to Muslims and historically is as much an Arab city as a Jewish one. His wish was to pray in the Al Aqsa Mosque, built by Caliph Abdul Melik (685-706), who also built the Dome of the Rock.[2]

The death of King Faisal, however, certainly did not end the Islamic commitment to the Holy City. In June, 1979, a German newspaper published this report.

> King Khaled and the princes, including the crown prince and his influential brothers, have agreed on a political strategy in the last few weeks which assigns the House of the Sauds and its kingdom a national and religious mission and gives new unity to the whole clan of princes. Their concern centers on Jerusalem. "We will spare no effort in realizing the claims of the Arab-Islamic nation on Jerusalem," stated inter-

nal minister Prince Naif in Tunis. Before that, King Khaled, and the Crown Prince had sworn, "If Jerusalem demands martyrs, we are ready."

Other considerations are secondary to the newly awakened religious zeal. If ties with America or Russia need to be weakened to strengthen the Arab influence on Jerusalem, they will do it. Only Islamic Arabs are to rule over Jerusalem and Palestine. That is what is meant when there is talk of "a just and comprehensive peace settlement concerning Jerusalem and the rights of the Palestinians."

In the West this new turn and the sharpening of developments in the Middle East which resulted have not been fully understood. From the old cities of Mecca and Medina the Saudis are again marching toward Jerusalem under the green banner of Islam—but just verbally at the moment. But should we think for a moment that they are not serious, they say with a slight smile, as a sheik did to this reporter in Jidda, "We have the oil—you can work for us."[3]

According to Islamic teachings, Jerusalem will play a key role in the end times. A great seducer (quite similar to the Antichrist mentioned in the Bible) will appear and Jesus will come down from heaven to destroy him. All remaining people will then be assimilated into the Muslim community, and two trumpet blasts will be heard: The first will announce the end of this age to those still living, and the second will awaken the dead. The final judgment will then take place in which God will review the deeds of each person. Every word and action will be weighed, and only those who can repeat the Islamic confession of faith will be able to stand before God. Unbelievers will suffer forever in hell's fires while believers will go to heaven where they will enjoy paradise for all eternity.

Moriah

For thousands of years, the center of Jerusalem has been Mount Moriah. It is believed that Abraham took Isaac up this same mountain four thousand years ago to offer him as a sacrifice as the Lord had directed. Later, "Then Solomon began to build the House of the LORD at Jerusalem in Mount Moriah, where the LORD had appeared to his Father David, at the place that David had prepared in the threshing floor of Ornan the Jebusite" (2 Chron. 3:1).

Sacrifices were made on this site for centuries according to the law of Moses until the Son of God came to do away with the need for a sacrifice by offering Himself as a sacrifice for us. Since the believer is sanctified for all eternity through the supreme sacrifice of Jesus, the temple with its sacrifices can no longer be justified.

> "Then after the sixty-two weeks the Messiah will be cut off and have nothing, and the people of the prince who is to come will destroy the city and the sanctuary. And its end will come with a flood; even to the end there will be war; desolations are determined" (Dan. 9:26).

Yet as the end times approach, Moriah will become significant again, for it is here that a world-dominating

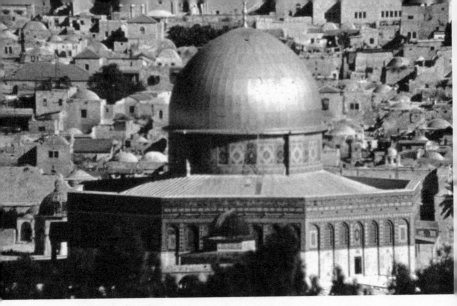

The Dome of the Rock in Jerusalem. Anyone wishing to enter must remove his shoes, not to spare the rugs, but to show reverence to Allah. Many a Christian tourist would go through with this only with a guilty conscience if he knew what was written in Arabic on the frieze surrounding the bottom of the dome: "There is no God but Allah! Praised be Allah who never produced a son nor had a companion nor needed a protector. Praise His greatness!"

power will reside. Mount Moriah witnessed many sacrifices, carried out according to the Law, which were foreshadowings of the coming of the Lamb of God who took away the sin of the world.

Today one of the wonders of the world stands on Mount Moriah: The Dome of the Rock, admired by Christians, Muslims, and Jews. On the frieze under the Dome one can read the Islamic confession of faith written in beautiful Arabic writing: *"La illah illa Allah"* ("There is no God but Allah"). The following verses from the Koran are also on the frieze.

146

O ye people of the Book! overstep not bounds in your religion; and of God, speak only truth. The Messiah, Jesus, son of Mary, is only an apostle of God, and his Word which he conveyed into Mary, and a Spirit proceeding from himself. Believe therefore in God and his apostles, and say not, "Three:" (there is a Trinity)— Forbear—it will be better for you. God is only one God! Far be it from His glory that He should have a son! His, whatever is in the Heavens, and whatever is in the Earth! And God is a sufficient Guardian (sura 4:169).

"And the peace of God was on me the day I was born, and will be the day I shall die, and the day I shall be raised to life." This is Jesus, the son of Mary; this is a statement of the truth concerning which they doubt. It beseemeth not God to beget a son. Glory be to Him! when he decreeth a thing, He only saith to it, Be, and it Is. And verily, God is my Lord and your Lord; adore Him then. This is the right way (sura 19:33–36).

Truly, this inscription should give us food for thought. Is it not the dreadful speech of the one who will rebel against everything of God's and against the Creator Himself? These selections from the Koran contradict God's inspired Word. One of the most important Islamic tenets is an explicit denial of the Trinity.

Temple of God or Abomination of Desolation?

When Paul wrote his epistle to the Thessalonians, the temple was still standing in Jerusalem, and Paul certainly had no reason to believe it would be destroyed. Prophetically he saw the man of sin in the temple when he said, "he sits as God in the temple of God, showing himself that he is God" (2 Thess. 2:4).

He was saying what Daniel said when he prophesied that the Beast would desecrate the holy place and an "abomination of desolation" would replace it. Jesus referred to Daniel's prophecy, too.

> "Therefore when you see the 'abomination of desolation,' spoken of by Daniel the prophet, standing in the holy place" (whoever reads, let him understand), "then let those who are in Judea flee to the mountains" (Matt. 24:15,16; see also Mark 13:14).

But more important than the Dome of the Rock itself, which stands on the site of the former temple, is the spirit that will reign there.

Some predict that a new temple will be built. But it is utopian to await the destruction of the Dome of the Rock and the Al Aqsa Mosque so that the temple can be rebuilt. As long as Islam exists, its followers will not allow another edifice to be constructed on that site. If we count on the reconstruction of the temple, we must assume the demise of Islam and the oil countries, as well as the rise of a new power. This would push the end times quite far into the future, contradicting other signs indicating the imminent return of Christ. At present there is no power on earth capable of dislodging the Muslims from the Temple Square in Jerusalem.

The temple of Israel has been replaced by a building

which is ruled by the spirit of antichrist, a power which will seduce the world for a time and, if possible, even lead astray the elect. He will offer the world riches, affluence, food, and survival. Today the call of the *muezzin* (the crier) is heard five times daily over the hill of Moriah: *"Allah hu akbar, Allah hu akbar"* ("Allah is the most high God").

There will be a battle that will rage at the Temple Square which will be a battle against Jesus Christ, the living Temple who was destroyed and raised up again in three days (see Matt. 26:61). The Dome of the Rock is a symbol of rebellion against Christ and His church.

There are deep mysteries here which may better be understood as we hold fast to God's Word. Everything revolves around God's temple, materially, intellectually, and spiritually. The visible should draw our attention to the spiritual. Paul describes the man of sin as one "who opposes and exalts himself above all that is called God or that is worshiped, so that he sits as God in the temple of God, showing himself that he is God" (2 Thess. 2:4).

It is important to realize the exact sense of the Moslem saying *Allah hu akbar* and the confession of faith. The Koran shuts Christ out from His position as the only Mediator between God and man. Daniel wrote about this system:

> "Then the king will do as he pleases, and he will exalt and magnify himself above every god, and will speak monstrous things against the God of gods; and he will prosper until the indignation is finished, for that which is decreed will be done" (Dan. 11:36).

Jerusalem and the Times of the Gentiles

For four thousand years Jerusalem has been an important location in God's dealings with man. And it will continue to play an important role, for in the closing chapters of the Bible, the apostle John saw a New Jerusalem illuminated by the glory of God.

> And I, John, saw the holy city, New Jerusalem, coming down from God out of heaven, prepared as a bride adorned for her husband. . . . And he carried me away in the Spirit to a great and high mountain, and showed me the great city, the holy Jerusalem, descending out of heaven from God (Rev. 21:2,10).

In the Olivet Discourse, Jesus makes an important statement regarding the future of Jerusalem: ". . . 'And Jerusalem will be trampled by the Gentiles until the times of the Gentiles are fulfilled' " (Luke 21:24). When Jesus said this, Jerusalem was being "trampled by the Gentiles," for it was under Roman rule. And it has been that way for nearly two thousand years. In fact, it wasn't until the first week of June, 1967, that the Old City of Jerusalem, to which Jesus referred, was truly governed by Jews. That was the first time Jerusalem had been under the control of an independent Israel since 597 B.C. And it wasn't until July, 1980, that the united Jerusalem was declared to be the "eternal" capital of Israel.

Truly the "times of the Gentiles" have come to an end. And with it will come the rise of the False Prophet, for the restraining work of the Holy Spirit will be taken away. Fierce battles will arise and rumors of war will be heard.

It is imperative that we decide now whose side we are on: Mohammed's or Christ's, Ishmael's or Isaac's.

7

Jesus Christ and the Antichrist

> Little children, it is the last hour; and as you have heard that the Antichrist is coming, even now many antichrists have come, by which we know that it is the last hour (1 John 2:18).

> . . . and every spirit that does not confess that Jesus Christ has come in the flesh is not of God. And this is the spirit of the Antichrist, which you have heard was coming, and even now it is already in the world (1 John 4:3).

The word *antichrist* is used only by John in his letters, but it refers to a man of wickedness who shall appear at the end times and who is described throughout the Bible. He opposes God and will exalt "himself above all that is called God or that is worshiped" (2 Thess. 2:4). Paul calls him "the son of perdition" (2 Thess. 2:3) and "the lawless one" (2 Thess. 2:9). Daniel describes him as a king who " '. . . will exalt himself, and magnify himself above every god, and will speak monstrous things against the God of gods . . .' " (Dan. 11:36).

In Revelation 13:11–18 he is pictured as a beast who "performs great signs," deceiving "those who dwell on the earth" and has the power to kill those who will not worship the image of the Beast.

The spirit of antichrist has been present since before the time of Christ in evil men and systems that have opposed God, His Word, and His people. When Antiochus Epiphanes sacrificed a pig on the altar in Jerusalem in the second century before Christ, bringing on the Maccabean revolt, he was displaying the spirit of antichrist. When Titus destroyed Jerusalem in A.D. 70 and dragged the holy objects and the great golden candlestick from the Temple through the streets of Rome, he was displaying the spirit of antichrist. When Hitler declared open season on Jews during World War II, he was displaying the spirit of antichrist.

But in the end times the anti-Christian spirit will take shape as a political and religious system directed by *one man*—the Antichrist. Never before have the world political, economic, moral, and religious conditions been as favorable for the Beast and False Prophet as they are today.

Christ and the Antichrist

The Scripture clearly explains the differences between Christ and the Antichrist. At the time of Jesus' baptism, God's voice came from heaven saying, " 'You are My beloved Son; in You I am well pleased' " (Luke 3:22). And later this was reiterated at Christ's transfiguration. Peter, an eyewitness at the transfiguration, explained what happened:

> For we have not followed cunningly devised fables when we made know to you the power

153

and coming of our Lord Jesus Christ, but were eyewitnesses of His majesty. For He received from God the Father honor and glory when such a voice came to Him from the Excellent Glory: "This is My beloved Son, in whom I am well-pleased." And we heard this voice which came from heaven when we were with Him on the holy mountain (2 Pet. 1:16–18).

Christ is shown in the Scriptures to be the sinless Son of God who came to redeem the world.

The Antichrist, however, is shown to be one who denies that Jesus is the Son of God. He is a liar.

. . . no lie is of the truth. Who is a liar but he who denies that Jesus is the Christ? He is antichrist who denies the Father and the Son. Whoever denies the Son does not have the Father either; he who acknowledges the Son also has the Father (1 John 2:21–23).

Whoever does not acknowledge the authority of the Word of God does not know truth from error. Only those who have the "spirit of wisdom" (see Eph. 1:17) are able to test the spirits.

Beloved, do not believe every spirit, but test the spirits, whether they are of God; because many false prophets have gone out into the world. By this you know the Spirit of God: Every spirit that confesses that Jesus Christ has come in the flesh is of God, and every spirit that does not confess that Jesus Christ has come in the flesh is not of God. And this is the spirit of the Antichrist, which you have heard was coming, and even now it is already in the world. You are of God, little children, and have overcome them, because He who is in you is greater than he who is in the world. They are of the world. Therefore they speak as of the world, and the world hears them. We are of God. He who knows God hears us; he who is not of God does not hear us. By this we know the spirit of truth and the spirit of error (1 John 4:1–6).

Not accepting God's authority leaves one open for every type of error. However, the Bible has clearly distinguished between Christ and the Antichrist. And the person who doesn't believe in the Son of God but follows the spirit of antichrist will find that "the wrath of God abides on him" (John 3:36).

The Pioneer: Liberal Theology

According to Scripture a significant characteristic of the Antichrist is his denial that Jesus Christ is the Son of the living God. Mohammed denied that Jesus is God's Son thirteen hundred years ago, but few in the West accepted his teachings. According to the Koran, Jesus is merely a messenger—no more. He is not *the* Word of God (*Kalimat Allah*) but is only a person who is bringing a word from God *(Kalam min Allah)*, a description that fits every other prophet including Mohammed himself. The statement from the Koran "Allah is the one and only eternal God. He does not beget, was not begotten, and none is his equal" draws a clear line between the Koran and the Bible.

It is fascinating to see how events are unrolling according to a definite plan. They seem to be synchronized and heading to a climax. Consider the nature of recent changes in the economy, in armaments, and in theology. For example, Christians in the West would not have considered denying the divinity of Christ one thousand years ago, but today it is accepted by some. By forsaking biblical foundations, the West has paved the way for the anti-Christian power of Islam.

Gerhard Bergman put his finger on the source of much unsound theology.

> The real cause of the spreading distortions in theology and church activities is to be found in the broken relationships of our churches to the Holy Scriptures. If we could answer the question of the cause with one phrase only, we would have to say: Biblical criticism.[1]

Unfortunately, the opinion of Christ expressed by Dr. Heinz Zahrnt is all too prevalent today.

> New Testament documents leave no doubt that Jesus was a real person, not a heavenly being. Nothing superhistorical, supernatural or unnatural can be found in him.[2]

While liberal theology has too often denied the deity of Christ, believing Christians have tended to look upon such denials with indignation, failing to realize how the devil can use them to influence vast numbers of people who are not Christians. This is shown very

clearly, however, in a brochure published by an Islamic mission for Europe in which the writer uses the
statements of liberal, so-called Christian theologians
to prove his point that Allah is the one true god and the
Koran is Allah's revelation to mankind. In describing
Christianity and Christ, the author says,

> The foundation of the Christian churches are the
> Gospels of the New Testament. Before we turn
> to these books, let us quote two prominent Pro-
> testant scholars. Professor Albert Schweitzer
> said once, "The New Testament Gospels, which
> report on the life of Jesus, are not suitable mate-
> rial for historic research." And Professor
> Bornkamm has stated that the whole genealogy
> of Christ as given in the New Testament, which
> the individual Gospels disagree on anyway, is
> not tenable because "it is too overgrown with
> legends and thoughts of Jewish and Christian
> Messianic dogma."[3]

The author runs no risks in quoting such "Christian"
authorities.

> From what we have already seen, one can con-
> clude that a considerable portion of the New
> Testament consists of writings which are *not* of
> Apostolic origin.

> Modern theology is of a similar opinion. In 1906
> Albert Schweitzer said, "The Jesus of Nazareth
> who came as the Messiah, proclaimed the King-
> dom of God, and died to consecrate his work,
> never existed. He is a figure designed by ration-

alism, enlivened by liberalism and clothed in a historic costume by modern theology. Our relationship to Jesus is fundamentally mystical."

This statement by the great humanitarian, jungle doctor, and theologian is a clear, unmistakable declaration of bankruptcy concerning Christology. Schweitzer recognized after two years of intensive work that all the efforts spent in attempting to prove the authenticity of the New Testament were in vain. Nevertheless he believed that the Nazarene lived and preached an ethic well suited to the historic situation of the Jews, complete with predictions of the end of the world.[4]

It is questionable if Schweitzer wanted to be understood this way.

Schweitzer thereby joins David Friedrich Strauss, who had said in 1840 that ancient myths were concentrated in the figure, the history, and the symbols of Jesus. Moreover, we have known since 1947 that the church sacraments were not instituted by Jesus, but were practiced 250 years earlier by the sect of the Essenes. In fact, there is an uncanny similarity between the teachings of this unique sect and the theological concepts of Christian denominations. For these reasons a large number of scholars have come to the conclusion that Jesus of Nazareth never existed! We cannot agree with this. Jesus lived, and he was the Abbot of Qumran (an Essene monastery), who called himself "teacher of righteousness."[5]

It is sad that this writer propagating Islam has to battle theologians who call themselves "Christians" over whether Jesus even existed. And we should certainly mention that neither Jesus Himself nor any of His disciples nor a Pharisee nor a Sadducee ever called Jesus the "Abbot of Qumran." Not even Josephus Flavius, the historian, used this term. Quoting again from the Islamic brochure:

> To be sure, Jesus was baptized by the Essene John, but he himself never baptized. Neither did he ever institute foot washing or the Last Supper. He never set himself up as judge of the world, nor did he ever claim to be the son of almighty God.

> On the contrary, as notable authorities have determined, he never called himself the Messiah. However, he calls himself "Son of Man" 69 times in the New Testament—a term that means "man" in Aramaic.[6]

Caiaphas the High Priest tore his robe when Jesus confirmed that He was God's Son. And yet as a true follower of Allah, the writer of the pamphlet must deny these facts and try to reduce Jesus to human status!

> Jesus of Nazareth was a man, albeit a noble one—a prophet. He confirmed that on a visit to his home town of Nazareth, where he said in front of all the people, "A prophet has no honor in his own country."

The best known Christologist of the 20th century, Professor Ethelbert Stauffer, comes close to the truth about Jesus when he says that based on historical research it is very probable that Jesus was a rebel preacher of brotherly love who was against the theocracy of the priests. Indeed all prophets were itinerant preachers. Exceptions were Moses and Mohammed, who were sent as bearers of the Law. All prophets turned against the dogmatic attitudes of the ruling classes of their times, proclaimed the wrath of God, and cried out for contemplation, repentance, humility, and prayer.

Did not Jesus Himself say, " 'I have come in My Father's name, and you do not receive Me; if another comes in his own name, him you will receive' " (John 5:43)?

We must emphasize here that not every word of the New Testament can be regarded as a forgery in the sense of a deliberate distortion. Rather, the Dead Sea scrolls prove that the Church's liturgy and sacraments did not originate with Jesus but were copies from the Essenes. In simple terms, they are of human, not divine origin.[7]

The author bases his comments on Stauffer's hypotheses, which can in no way be proved. He continues:

What is left, then, of Christianity, and what the Church ascribes to Jesus? Jesus alone remains—his person is geniune. God's blessing was on him.

But in this historical chaos who shall answer questions about the life, work, and mission of the Nazarene sent from God? It is the holy one who came from Paran [Mohammed], about whom Jesus said, "I still have many things to say to you, but you cannot bear them now. However, when He, the Spirit of truth has come, He will guide you into all truth; for He will not speak on His own authority, but whatever He hears He will speak; and He will tell you things to come." It was Mohammed who brought the world the final laws of God, the good news for all believers.[8]

The Islamic writer applied Jesus' words about the coming of the Holy Spirit to Mohammed. If Jesus had wanted to talk of Mohammed, He would have made it much clearer. The author is interpreting this passage from John's gospel according to the Koran's teachings.

Contemporaries and the "New Testament" can in no way present a credible picture of Jesus. Stauffer says, "In the history of the Church there has not yet been an unbiased report on the life of Jesus of Nazareth; not even one."

Having recognized this, let us make an unprejudiced attempt at examining the witness of the Koran. We must remember that the holy book appeared at a time when the struggle for the Christian (i.e. Nazarene-Jewish) canon had reached a climax: the 7th century. Is it any wonder that we Muslims believe the revelation of the Koran is a direct intervention of God?[9]

Clearly this author is preaching another gospel, and Paul stated forcefully that those who do such things should "be accursed" (Gal. 1:8). It is true that Jesus calls Himself the Son of Man, but there are also forty-seven passages in the New Testament where He is called the Son of God. The writer has taken from the New Testament only what fits his purposes. His message, therefore, is not credible.

The Muslims continually reproach Christians for having a "falsified New Testament," but where is the correct one? They say the whole truth is in the Koran. They claim the Koran is the light that will lead men out of darkness. How can a person who calls himself a Christian possibly come to terms with such a viewpoint? David said, "In Thy light we see light" (Ps. 36:9) and Isaiah said, "Woe to those who call evil good, and good evil . . ." (Is. 5:20). Theologians who deny the basic doctrines of Christian truth—especially the fact that Jesus Christ is the Son of God—are supplying Muslims with support for their teaching and are guilty of calling good evil.

If Christians are going to be ready to defend themselves against the attacks of anti-Christian teaching—especially since the church is in a weakened position due to the undermining of basic doctrines by its own theologians—we must be aware of the points of attack.

Periklytos and Parakletos

Islamic doctrine states that Jesus predicted the coming of Mohammed when He said, "And I will pray the Father, and He will give you another Helper, that He may abide with you forever" (John 14:16). The Greek word translated "helper" or "comforter" is *parakletos* and refers to the coming of the Holy Spirit. However, Muslims claim that the word was originally *periklytos*, meaning "the praised one," which is similar to the Arabic name Ahmed—or Mohammed. Jesus is quoted in the Koran as saying:

> . . . "O children of Israel! of a truth I am God's apostle to you to confirm the law which was given before me, and to announce an apostle that shall come after me whose name shall be Ahmad" . . . (sura 61:6)!

Jesus' words are made to refer to Mohammed. The Holy Spirit is excluded. Muslims even say that the words "Holy Spirit" were added to John's Gospel at a later time and that they distort Jesus' message. Rather, they teach that Jesus spoke of a leader whom people would follow after Jesus left the visible world. He could not have meant a spirit, they say, because a spirit can neither hear nor speak. The *periklytos* is a human being, a prophet sent from God, who would hear God's voice and proclaim it to mankind.

Islamic teachers are doing exactly what some theologians have done. They claim that some of Jesus' statements are false or were added later and other statements, because they agree with their theories, are authentic. This was necessary to make Jesus appear to announce the coming of Mohammed.

If one claims, as Muslims do, that a spirit can neither hear nor speak, he is not merely misinterpreting John 14:16 but calling God Himself into question, for "God is Spirit, and those who worship Him must worship

Him in spirit and truth" (John 4:24). This would mean that God could neither hear nor speak. Our lives therefore would be led by chance.

The teaching that God is spirit is found not only in John's Gospel, but in Acts, the writings of Paul, and in numerous Old Testament passages as well. Yet Islam rejects all of these. The last time I was in Africa a *faki* (teacher of the Koran) told me that Paul was simply a Jew who forged Scripture; therefore his writings could be ignored. The teaching that God is spirit is only one point at which the Bible is a mystery and a stumbling-block to Muslims.

If Islam uses such faulty reasoning to claim the right to consider the Koran the authentic confirmation of the Old and New Testaments—a revelation to Mohammed by the angel Gabriel—how much more, based on the internal witness of the Bible itself, does the Christian have the right to claim that the Bible is inspired by God's Spirit!

Mohammed, and with him the whole Islamic world, is convinced that he was the promised *periklytos*, the praised one. He claims to be the "spirit of truth" who will teach mankind all things and lead them into all truth.

Jesus, the Son of God

Islam not only denies the existence of the Holy Spirit but also the divinity of Jesus. There is no anti-Christian power in the world that denies the sonship of Christ and His death on the cross so distinctly and consistently as Islam.

For the Muslim it is an abomination to confess and believe that Jesus Christ is the Son of God. I have seen Muslims spit on the ground, saying, "Allah, forgive me for having heard such a thing." To say that God has a son is, for them, blasphemy.

> Infidels now are they who say, "Verily God is the Messiah Ibn Maryam [son of Mary]! SAY: And who could aught obtain from God, if he chose to destroy the Messiah Ibn Maryam, and his mother, and all who are on the earth together (sura 5:19)?

Islam teaches that Jesus was a prophet, as was Isaiah and Mohammed. But the Bible says that Jesus is God's Son, whom God "has appointed heir of all things, by whom also He made the worlds" (Heb. 1:2). The Bible teaches that by Jesus Christ all things were created and that he existed eternally before He became a man (see Col. 1:15–17). This is unacceptable to a Muslim.

Whoever believes Jesus is the Son of God is considered an unbeliever by Muslims. To them Jesus is only a created being. The Muslim cannot understand the thoughts of God (see 1 Cor. 2:14) because for him the world, paradise, and eternity are only sensual. Although he praises Allah as the Almighty One, he does not believe that Allah could intervene in the course of nature and send Jesus, the eternally existing One, into time.

> And they say, "God hath a son:" No! Praise be to Him! But—His, whatever is in the Heavens and the Earth! All obeyeth Him (sura 2:110).

And SAY: Praise be to God who hath not begotten a son, who hath no partner in the Kingdom,
nor any protector on account of weakness. And
magnify him by proclaiming His greatness (sura
17.111).

Jesus, the Redeemer

Islam also denies the biblical teaching that "the
blood of Jesus Christ His Son cleanses us from all sin"
(1 John 1:7). Scripture says, "In Him [Jesus Christ] we
have redemption through His blood, the forgiveness
of sins, according to the riches of His grace" (Eph. 1:7).
But a Muslim spokesman says,

Be certain that your faith in the blood of Jesus is
in vain. Had he been crucified not just once, but a
thousand times, he could not have saved you.
Salvation lies in faith, in love, and in certainty;
not in the blood of a human being![10]

Here we see the poison of the serpent! The Koran
regards the biblical message of salvation as a lie, a
fable. And since there is no more fanatical religion in
the world than Islam, the unarmed Christian church in
the West will be overrun in the coming strife. The
battle before us is not primarily an economic one, but a
spiritual one. We are in danger because Christianity
has never been as lukewarm and weak as it is today.

Put on the whole armor of God, that you may be
able to stand against the wiles of the devil. For
we do not wrestle against flesh and blood, but
against principalities, against powers, against

the rulers of the darkness of this age, against spiritual wickedness in the heavenly places (Eph. 6:11,12).

Jesus in the Koran

The Koran mentions Abraham and the Old Testament patriarchs, Jesus, Mary, and others from the New Testament and asserts that all these people were servants of Allah. But the Koran is in error not only in claiming that Allah is the god of these biblical figures but also in the way it twists history. It mixes truth and falsehood. But Muslims, 650 million strong, believe it is the absolute truth and that the Bible is absolutely false.

The Koran (sura 3.31 ff.) says that Mary the mother of Jesus was the daughter of Imran and an unnamed woman. Mohammed confused Imran with Amran in the Old Testament and Mary with Miriam for he says that Mary was Aaron's sister (sura 19:29). The Bible says Amran was the father of Moses, Aaron, and Miriam. Mohammed says Mary was dedicated to Allah while still in her mother's womb and was brought up not at home but in the temple, nourished miraculously by Allah.

In a "place toward the East" where Mary went into seclusion, an angel proclaimed Allah's plan to her: He would bless her with a "holy son" (sura 19:19). She protested that she was an unmarried virgin, but she could not escape the situation for it was "a thing decreed" (v. 21). Thus she conceived Jesus through a divine act of creation.

To escape slanderous tongues, she "retired with

him to a far-off place" (v. 22). She gave birth to Jesus under a palm tree and was consoled during the birth pangs by a voice from beneath her, saying, "Grieve not thou thy Lord hath provided a streamlet at thy feet:—And shake the trunk of the palm-tree toward thee: it will drop fresh ripe dates upon thee" (v. 25).

When she returned home, she was greeted by reproaches from her relatives. But she pointed to the Christ Child and did not try to defend herself. The Child immediately began to talk and proclaimed Himself a slave and prophet of Allah (sura 19:31ff.). This miracle was His first message to men and a justification of His mother.

Mohammed does not seem to have a very accurate picture of the life and works of Jesus. He said that Jesus was sent to the Jews as a prophet, first to confirm the Torah and to revise it (sura 3:43ff.), then to bring them the gospel (sura 3:43). By the term "gospel," however, Mohammed did not mean the message of salvation as we find it in the New Testament. Rather, he taught that a divine revelation was given to Jesus like the one he said was given to him in the Koran. He assumed the two were in agreement.

The Christian gospel is a false gospel in the eyes of Muslims because they refuse to acknowledge Jesus as the Son of God and refuse to see His uniqueness apart from other prophets. Jesus is seen as merely one in a long line of prophets from Allah. This is certainly different from the biblical position found in Hebrews 1:1–4.

> God, who at various times and in different ways
> spoke in time past to the fathers by the prophets,

has in these last days spoken to us by His Son, whom He has appointed heir of all things, by whom also He made the world; who being the brightness of His glory and the express image of His person, and upholding all things by the word of His power, when He had by Himself purged our sins, sat down at the right hand of the Majesty on high, having become so much better than the angels, as He has by inheritance obtained a more excellent name than they.

Christ and Mohammed

Islam has set itself squarely against Christian teaching by denying that Jesus is the Son of God, by denying that salvation comes through Jesus Christ alone, by denying that God is a spirit, and by making Jesus' promise of the Holy Spirit refer to Mohammed. Clearly Islam displays the spirit of antichrist.

"Mohammed went the way of human success," said Pascal. "Jesus went the way of human destruction." Jesus is the Son of God; Mohammed is a follower of the devil. Satan offered Jesus an earthly kingdom, but He turned it down.

And the devil, taking Him up on a high mountain, showed Him all the kingdoms of the world in a moment of time. And the devil said to Him, "All this authority I will give You, and their glory; for that has been delivered to me, and I give it to whomever I wish. Therefore, if You will worship before me, all will be Yours" (Luke 4:5–7).

Jesus refused Satan's offer, which, although it sounded tempting, was merely an offer to exchange time for eternity. If he had accepted it, Jesus would have been in Satan's power and the church would never have been born. Jesus knew about eternity and the glories of heaven.

Mohammed, on the other hand, who came in his own name and was temporal, knew nothing of eternity and therefore accepted Satan's offer. The Islamic community is now in power because Satan is keeping his promise. We are seeing not just a clash between Christ and Mohammed, but a clash between the Christ and the spirit of antichrist.

The Antichrist

Just as Jesus shall be "revealed from heaven with His mighty angels" (2 Thess. 1:7), so the Antichrist also will be visibly revealed (2 Thess. 2:8,9). "And the dragon gave him his power, his throne, and great authority" (Rev. 13:2). Just as God the Father received glory through His risen Son, so shall Satan receive veneration from mankind through the Beast. "And they worshiped the dragon who gave authority to the beast; and they worshiped the beast, saying, "Who is like the beast? Who is able to make war with him?" (Rev. 13:4).

The age of the Antichrist has already begun. Mankind has become materialistic, worshiping a golden calf, not willing to make personal sacrifices of any kind. Thus men are unable to react properly to the challenges of the world situation. Soon they will be bowing before the False Prophet and the Beast.

By taking a position against Israel, the West has rejected its foundation and its spiritual heritage. We have chosen, as did Sarah and Abraham, the second best way, the way of the human will and fleshly desires. This way of thinking has been forming over a long time, has had much time to degenerate, and will be extremely difficult to change.

Throughout the history of the church, speculation has been made concerning the identity of the Antichrist. The conjecture has often been made that he would come from Rome. J. A. Bengel, for instance, wrote,

> From the very beginning we have awaited an enemy who would bring about disastrous events under the guise of righteousness. It is customary to call him "the great Antichrist." If the Beast is not the Roman papacy, a power will have to be found that is greater than the Pope.

He believes the Beast is Rome, but he doesn't exclude the possibility of a stronger power. Today the strength of the papacy pales before that of the Middle Eastern oil countries.

One of the key characteristics of the Antichrist is that he denies that Jesus Christ is the Son of God. Therefore, if we look for the Antichrist in the Roman Catholic church, we are making a mistake; Rome has never denied the sonship of Jesus. It fits the facts better to say that the Antichrist will arise out of Islam.

Others have thought that the Antichrist would be a Jew, for he will direct a spiritual power that will seduce the world, especially those nations bordering on Israel. The Antichrist will be a son of Abraham, a Semite, but we must remember that two families grew out of Abraham: the Arabs as well as the Jews. The one line is led by Satan and is preparing future chaos. The other will be led by the Spirit of Christ and is preparing the rapture of the church and coming glory. It will bring about the destruction of the Antichrist with the binding of the Dragon, the Beast, and the False Prophet so that the thousand-year reign of Jesus Christ can begin.

The Anti-Christian Prince of Peace

It is the wish of every Muslim to pray once in his life in the Al Aqsa mosque. President Sadat fulfilled this wish in late 1977. Here was a visible demonstration of the successful efforts for peace. The whole world looked on by television as the "prince of peace" rode triumphantly into Jerusalem. One reporter said, "It is as if the Messiah were coming!"

Then the world watched as Sadat cried out to Allah in the Al Aqsa mosque, *"Allah il Allah"* and *"Allah hu akbar"* ("Allah is the most high God"). People wept for joy in front of their television screens. Israelis danced in the streets of Jerusalem. Had the moment of reconciliation between the two brothers finally come? Had the Middle East crisis finally been solved?

This scene of Sadat in Jerusalem was just the dress rehearsal for the strong man the Middle East is waiting for. What will it be like when he marches into Jerusalem and establishes himself in the "abomination of desolation"? He will worship his god there, not the Father of our Lord Jesus Christ. This strong man will deny that Jesus is the Son of God.

Let no one deceive you by any means; for that Day will not come unless the falling away comes first, and the man of sin is revealed, the son of perdition, who opposes and exalts himself above all that is called God or that is worshipped, so that he sits as God in the temple of God, showing himself that he is God.

And then the lawless one will be revealed, whom the Lord will consume with the breath of His mouth and destroy with the brightness of His coming (2 Thess. 2:3,4,8).

In other words, a man will come, taking the place of Christ by claiming lordship over everything. He will be the enemy of all who bear the name of Jesus. It is a frightening fact that from the very holiest place, the dwelling place of the God of Israel, messengers of the False Prophet will call for the destruction of Israel.

Satan has always tried—and will never stop trying—to wipe the Jewish race from the face of the earth. He did everything he could to prevent Israel from bringing forth the Savior; recall Herod's command to murder all Jewish babies in the Bethlehem region. And because the nation of Israel stands in the middle of God's plans for the end times, as well as being the center of the drama of the first coming of His son two thousand years ago, Satan's activities against Israel will increase. "He who has an ear, let him hear."

False Peace and True Peace

The convenant of peace that will be made according to Daniel's prophecy (see Dan. 9:27) and will be bro-

173

The Arabs await a powerful leader who will reunite the Arab states into a united Arab kingdom. This power figure will come near the end of time and rally the Islamic world.

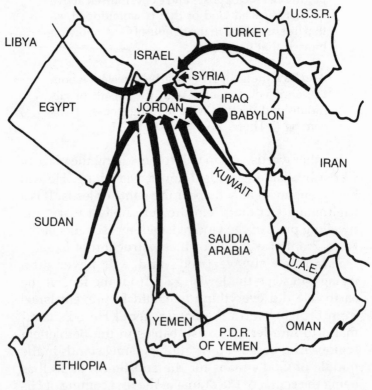

Babylon is the starting point of Daniel's prophecy, and it is in this area that the prophecy will be realized. It will not commence in Europe or Rome. Babylon endures as Babylon.

ken in the middle of the year of weeks (see Dan. 7:25) can only be a false peace (see Dan. 8:25). Its basis will be compromise and falsehood; it will be made with a demonic power under the guise of appealing to Abraham and monotheism.

> "For from the least of them even to the greatest of
>   them
> Every one is greedy for gain,
> And from the prophet even to the priest
> Every one deals falsely.
> And they have healed, the wound of my people
>   slightly,
> Saying, 'Peace, peace'; But there is no peace"
> (Jer. 6:13,14).

> . . . they have misled My people by saying,
> "Peace!" when there is no peace. And when
> anyone builds a wall, behold, they plaster it
> over with whitewash (Ezek. 13:10).

The peace negotiations of today are simply a whitewash which will be rinsed away in the coming Tribulation. The whitewashers will go to ruin and with them all the peoples who were seduced by them. Peace cannot be made on the basis of lies.

Any peace concluded today can only be a marriage between Israel and a bridegroom who marries her only to destroy her more easily. A lasting peace can only be made on the basis of truth contracted with the Prince of Peace Himself.

There will be no peace for Israel until it acknowledges the Prince of Peace, Jesus Christ. " 'If you had known, even you, especially in this your day [Oh Jerusalem], the things which belong to your peace!' " (Luke 19:42). How long will the truth remain hidden from Israel's eyes?

In the last days,
The mountain of the house of the LORD
Will be established as the chief of the moun-
    tains,
And will be raised above the hills;
And all the nations will stream to it.
And many peoples will come and say,
"Come, let us go up to the mountain of the LORD,
To the house of the God of Jacob;
That He may teach us concerning His ways,
And that we may walk in His paths."
For the law will go forth from Zion,
And the word of the LORD from Jerusalem.
And He will judge between the nations,
And will render decisions for many peoples;
And they will hammer their swords into plow-
    shares, and their spears into pruning hooks.
Nation will not lift up sword against nation,
And never again will they learn war (Is. 2:2–4).

The last part of Isaiah 2:4 has been taken by the United Nations as the goal of that world body. It is engraved in stone in a small park across the street from the organization's magnificent headquarters in New York City. But the members of the UN are trying to achieve world peace without acknowledging God's supremacy.

The King of Kings has been shut out of world history, and therefore we have the current Middle East problem. The ultimate goal of the anti-Christian power is the destruction of Israel. The peace that will be concluded with Israel will last, therefore, only "a time, times, and half a time" (Dan. 7:25).

The Gentile nations must go through the Tribulation along with Israel. It will be a tribulation such as the world has never seen. They will become humbled and recognize the Lord as King of Kings. The Tribulation will get worse and worse. When Israel and the nations see to what depths the prince of this world has brought them and that there is no way out, Jesus Himself will intervene.

> And then the sign of the Son of Man will appear in heaven, and then all the tribes of the earth will mourn, and they will see the Son of Man coming on the clouds of heaven with power and great glory (Matt. 24:30).

Then the King will rule from Jerusalem and His church with Him. This kingdom of peace will be born through the birth pangs of the great Tribulation.

Every alliance that Israel makes, except with God Himself, based on His Word, can only be a substitute solution, driving Israel further into a quagmire of desperation.

> "O Jerusalem, Jerusalem, the one who kills the prophets and stones those who are sent to her! How often I wanted to gather your children together, as a hen gathers her chicks under her wings, and you were not willing!
>
> "See! Your house is left to you desolate; for I say to you, you shall see Me no more till you say, Blessed is He who comes in the name of the Lord!" (Matt. 23:37-39).

The present peace with Egypt is not in accordance with God's will. "Woe to those who go down to Egypt for help, and rely on horses . . . but they do not look to the Holy One of Israel, nor seek the LORD!" (Is. 31:1). The true alliance will only come about when Zechariah's prophecy is fulfilled and the Lord is King of the whole earth: ". . . in that day the LORD will be the only one and His name the only one" (Zech. 14:9). Only then can Egypt, Syria, and Israel make a peace treaty—all of them protected and ruled by the Prince of Peace.

> In that day there will be a highway from Egypt to Assyria, and the Assyrians will come into Egypt and the Egyptians into Assyria, and the Egyptians will worship with the Assyrians. In that day Israel will be the third party with Egypt and Assyria, a blessing in the midst of the earth (Is. 19:23,24).

In that time of the millennial kingdom, Ishmael will find his way to Jehovah, and the peace treaty between the once estranged brothers of the Middle East will truly be a bond of brotherhood. The Sun of Righteousness will burn away the symbol of the crescent moon over the Middle East. The earth will join in the song of the psalmist, "From the rising of the sun to its setting, the name of the LORD is to be praised" (113:3). The nations will enter into peace in the name of Jehovah, not under the name of a foreign god.

> For from the rising of the sun, even to its setting,
> My name will be great among the nations . . .
> (Mal. 1:11).

8

The Four Beasts of the End Times

Daniel was a young Jewish man who was taken captive to Babylon from Israel in about 606 B.C. He and three others were picked to receive special training for service to the Babylonian king. They were offered many comforts appropriate for those serving in the royal court, but they refused to compromise their dedication to God. When the king, Nebuchadnezzar, had a dream that no wise man could interpret, Daniel, under God's guidance, provided the interpretation.

Daniel became an important person in the royal courts of the Babylonian and Persian Empires. He is best known for interpreting the mysterious handwriting that suddenly appeared on the wall where King Belshazzar of Babylon was holding a banquet, and for his surviving a night in a den of lions in which he was thrown for violating the royal edict of Darius, king of Media, by praying to God.

Daniel interpreted several dreams for others and records, in the Book of Daniel, a number of visions he had himself. In the first year of Belshazzar's reign, he had a vision in which "four great beasts came up from the sea." This vision was a prediction of future events, and the traditional interpretation is that the first beast represents the Babylonian Empire, the second the Media-Persian Empire, the third the Greek Empire, and the fourth the Roman Empire.

However, let me offer another interpretation that relates this vision of Daniel to the times in which we are living. In retrospect we can say with some certainty that the end times began with the Third Reich in Germany when the world focused attention once more on Israel. Therefore biblical prophecy dealing with the end times should relate very closely to what is happening in the news today. The following interpretation of the vision of four beasts in Daniel 7 is based on the *Encyclopédie Prophétique* by Jacques Levitan.

The First Beast

> "The first was like a lion and had the wings of an eagle. I kept looking until its wings were plucked, and it was lifted up from the ground, and made to stand on two feet like a man; a human mind also was given to it" (Dan. 7:4).

The first beast was like a lion (which in Hebrew is *ari* or *arieh* and sounds like *Aryan,* the name of Hitler's super race) and had wings like an eagle. The Hitler regime, the first beast, introduced the end times by attempting to annihilate the Jews. But, ironically, Hitler's activities paved the way for the creation of the state of Israel. After World War II, Germany was divided into two and became more sane (received a mind) again.

The conquest of Palestine was among the goals of Hitler. He wanted to carry his "Final Solution" into the heart of the Promised Land—the last hope of the Jewish people. The German army had the order to drive into Palestine from Egypt, to take the land and its capital. The German troops hoped to find gasoline in a British military camp in the north of Egypt. But when they overran the camp they found that the supplies were gone. Then they hoped to get fuel from an Italian ship; but instead of gasoline, it was filled with water! Enemy artillery brought the German drive to a standstill, the march on Jerusalem was stopped, and the retreat began. The first beast was not allowed to destroy Israel. Hitler said his Third Reich would last one thousand years, but it was a short one thousand years. His time was limited by God.

The Second Beast

> "And behold, another beast, a second one, re-sembling a bear. And it was raised up on one side, and three ribs were in its mouth between its teeth; and thus they said to it, 'Arise, devour much meat.'" (Dan. 7:5).

Russia, the second beast, is often portrayed as a bear and has certainly "devoured" the Eastern European countries. Immediately after Ben Gurion read the proclamation declaring the foundation of Israel, the new country was recognized by the Soviet Union. But today the Soviets are the firm allies of Israel's enemies, and they are playing the Arabs against Israel with great effectiveness.

Nearly three hundred years ago, Peter the Great of Russia prophesied that the future of the world would be bound up with the region around the Persian Gulf; he could not have known how indispensable oil would be today. He said, "Whoever controls the Persian Gulf will rule the world." That is why Saudi Arabia fears that the Soviet Union will want to expand its area of political and economic domination to the Middle East. After 1982, Russia will have to import oil to keep its machinery running. Thus it is not impossible that Russia will actively join in the battle against Israel as an ally of "Assyria" (Iraq and Syria), the fourth beast.

But the time of Russia, the second beast, is limited too.

The Third Beast

> After this I kept looking, and behold, another one, like a leopard, which had on its back four wings of a bird; the beast also had four heads, and dominion was given to it" (Dan. 7:6).

The third beast will be raised to power by the second, and its ascendancy marks the introduction of Islam onto the world stage. The third beast, Egypt under Nasser, is Islam beginning to flex its muscles. Nasser led the Middle East into new paths. He nationalized the Suez Canal, in the process demonstrating the West's impotence and disunity. He tried to unite the Arab world under the banner of Arab nationalism in order to rid the Arab territory of the "foreign body" (Israel).

Pan-Arabism and hatred of Israel are the common denominators which unite the Arabs. Nasser was the man of the hour. He successfully allied Syria, Jordan,

182

the Sudan, and Libya (four heads as mentioned in Daniel 7:6), plotted a war against Israel, and was supported by Russian air force and military advisers.

Nasser was the link between Pan-Arabism and Pan-Islamism. But Nasser's time was also limited; even he was but a transition figure to the fourth beast.

Before the Ayatollah Khomeini left Paris, he said: "Nothing but an Islamic republic is legitimate: neither the Shah's regime nor Bakhtiar's." Muslims believe that no rule or religion is legitimate except the one of Allah that shall rule the world: Islam.

> Babylon has been a golden cup in the hand of
>   the LORD,
> Intoxicating all the earth.
> The nations have drunk of her wine;
> Therefore the nations are going mad (Jer. 51:7).

The Fourth Beast: Rome or Babylon?

The traditional interpretation of the fourth beast in Daniel's vision is that it is the Roman Empire. Such commentators say that it refers to both the historic Roman Empire as well as a revived Roman Empire in the last days. They identify the revived empire with the prophecies concerning Babylon in Revelation (e.g., Rev. 17:1–7).

But there is no hint in the Bible that the earlier Roman Empire had a prophetic mission. It is a mistake to locate the prophetic Babylon in Rome, for that clouds the issue and prevents us from seeing the true nature of the fourth beast. Rather, the Mediterranean lands and a supposedly united Europe will be domi-

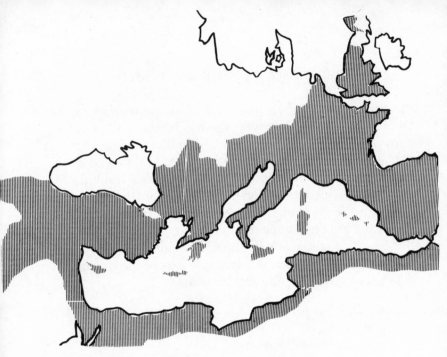

The ancient Roman Empire.

nated by the strong force from the Middle East. José Fralon said, "The oil embargo by the Arab countries made it clear to all Europeans that there is no united Europe."[1]

Today, Babylon (Iraq) is in commotion. The Baath movement, which has as its goal the unification of the Arab peoples, was born in this region. The word *Baath* means "resurrection." Iraq is dedicated to the annihilation of Israel, and it is an oil country that could become the leader of the Arab world. It could bring forth another Saladin (1138–1193) who would help the Arabs realize their dream of unification.

The Baath party, founded in Syria in 1941, knows that Islam is still the only power uniting

184

all Arabs. The reunification of all the Arab peoples in a Greater Arab Empire is the dream of Iraqi foreign policy. The beginning of this is supposed to be the union of Iraq and Syria in the near future. The Iraqis are so successful that they are already being called the Prussians of the Middle East.[2]

Babylon, the Old Testament city of Babel on the Euphrates, is supposed to be rebuilt, according to a resolution by the Iraqi government. It was announced Sunday in Baghdad that the estimate for the cost of this will be $360 million, to be paid by UNESCO. Archaeologists, as well as representatives of UNESCO and other international organizations, were reportedly invited to come and see the site for themselves about 57 miles south of Baghdad. The oldest remains can be traced back to the third millennium B.C. After the Persian conquest of 538 B.C., Babylon became the third capital of the Persian Empire.[3]

Perhaps the identification of the fourth beast with Rome by Western biblical commentators is to some degree caused by an unwillingness to believe that world leadership, whether good or evil, would ever reside outside of Europe.

The apostle John referred to the fourth beast when he said, " 'The beast that you saw was, and is not, and will ascend out of the bottomless pit . . .' " (Rev. 17:8). He saw the beast appear, and from that point on it did exercise great power, including the rise of Islam from 630 to 1683. After that time, however, the West dominated world events. "The beast . . . is not," it had lost

185

its power, it had become subservient. During the colonial period of the last several hundred years, the West controlled the world's fate.

The decline of the West started after the Second World War as one after another the colonies threw off the yoke of colonialism. Gradually the beast will gain the upper hand. It will not reign long, but it will reign violently and exploit all the power granted to it.

The Christian temporal authority, which began with Emperor Constantine and found expression in subsequent horrors, injustices, wars, persecutions of Jews (and Christians), and the Crusades, will receive its just reward for its whoring ways. The following reveals an example of "Christian" errors.

> In 842 the Khalif Mutasim died, and the Pope used the death notice to play a seemingly well-meant joke: overnight he transformed the Islamic bank into his own private financial institute and called it the "bank of the Holy Spirit," for He had, it was said, given him the idea.[4]

The beast already has the capacity to fully repay the West for past wrongdoings.

We are reaching the point where the future of the West lies completely in the hands of the beast. Since it has liberated itself from Western control, the beast is growing stronger. Godlessness is making itself more and more strongly felt.

Babylon

> ". . . and behold, a fourth beast, dreadful and terrifying and extremely strong; and it had large

iron teeth. It devoured and crushed, and trampled down the remainder with its feet; and it was different from all the beasts that were before it; and it had ten horns" (Dan. 7:7).

Babylonian Empire (2550–539 B.C.)
Assyrian Empire (539–331 B.C.)

The third beast was Egypt, which led modern Islamic nations to think about unity. But Egypt has now incurred the wrath of those nations because of its peace efforts with Israel. President Sadat of Egypt has been condemned in Damascus and other Islamic centers. The way has been paved for the fourth beast, ancient Babylon, which is today called Iraq, to unite ten kings under its flag. This alliance will bring forth the mightiest world ruler yet, one who is both "dreadful and extremely terrifying."

He will rule with the power given him by the dragon. Just as no one tried to stop the first beast's persecution of the Jews, no one will stand up to the fourth beast when he attempts to annihilate Israel and battle the saints (see Dan. 7:21 and Rev. 13:7). Just as an entire nation was led astray by the first beast (Hitler), the whole world will be led astray by the fourth. Whoever does not submit to him will be subdued and broken in pieces (see Dan. 7:23). He will control the very existence of the nations, and no one will be able to buy or sell goods or services without submitting to him (see Rev. 13:17).

What, then, can a small land like Israel with barely three million people do against the whole world? Nothing, in human terms, but God sees it otherwise.

> "Since you are precious in My sight,
>   Since you are honored and I love you,
>   I will give other men in your place
>   and other peoples in exchange
>   for your life" (Is. 43:4).

The world will be silent, even as it is today, not being

188

able to do otherwise when tyrants act. This fourth beast will appear in the night when the world is sleeping and unwilling to see the truth. This will be by far the worst of the beasts. For a time it will have success in attacking the Holy Land (see Dan. 7:25), for each beast receives a certain time in which to carry out its charge (see Dan. 7:12).

The first three beasts failed in their efforts to destroy Israel, and the fourth beast will not be successful either. The Son of Man (Jesus Christ) will appear in the clouds and will free the whole earth. Without God's intervention, the fourth beast would be successful in exterminating Israel, but the appearance of the Messiah will be Israel's salvation.

The last beast could only be Iraq. This empire is forming today. A union of Iraq, Syria, and Lebanon is not unthinkable. This territory is the cradle of civilization and, according to tradition, it is where the fall of man occurred. From this land came Nimrod (see Gen. 10:8), the first tyrant, a mighty hunter who forged the first weapons and built the first cities, including Babel and Nineveh (see Gen. 10:10,11).

From Nineveh came a forerunner of the Antichrist, Antiochus Epiphanes. Again and again it is clear that history repeats itself. Ancient Assyria is modern Iraq, and just as Assyria rose up against Israel in Old Testament times, it will do so again in the last days.

Sitting on a sea of oil, Iraq will stun the whole world. Nimrod was called "a mighty one in the earth," and from this same area will come the strong man of the future. "There is one come out of thee [Nineveh], that imagineth evil against the Lord, a wicked counselor" (Nah. 1:11, KJV). He will be an unknown person who will gain power through intrigues, conspiracies, and flatteries (see Dan. 11:21) for a length of time to be determined by the Lord. He will not only be a political leader, but a religious one as well. He will be arrogant and proud towards the Lord of Lords (see Dan. 11:36, 2 Thess. 2:4).

Do not forget that only the charisma and appeal of the Ayatollah Khomeini was necessary to topple the mighty dynasty of the Shah of Iran. Imagine what power there would be when Islam is led by "a mighty one on earth"!

The Lebanon crisis is also included in the plans for "Greater Syria." " 'Through your servants you have reproached the Lord, and you have said, "with my many chariots I came up to the heights of the mountains, to the remotest parts of Lebanon . . ." ' " (Is. 37:24). Do not be surprised when the Christians flee Lebanon and say there is no future for them in that country.

Ten kings will unite under the flag of the fourth beast, Iraq, and lead the world into its final chaos. The fourth beast will be allied with Russia, the second beast, and the Russians will supply arms and ammunition.

The Soviet Union is advancing the timetable in the Middle East, as is America. According to the usually reliable Egyptian newspaper *Ros el Jussuf*, the Palestinian terrorists are planning to increase their attacks on Israel. Cuban units will be transported from Angola, Ethiopia, and South Yemen to Syria. These units will prepare for the arrival of thousands of Cuban soldiers, pilots, and logistic experts. The Soviets are said to have asked for the transfer of fifteen thousand military experts to the Middle East.

Moscow's headquarters in the Middle East and Africa has moved from Aden to a secret location south of Tripoli in Libya. A Soviet marshall is at the head of a staff of Cuban, East German, and Czech officers.

Since Israel is the bone of contention, the whole world will attempt to rid itself of it. A peaceful solution seems more and more impossible. Israel is becoming lonelier and more forsaken; it will be able to count on no one in the final conflict except the Lord Himself.

Eventually the world will lament the fall of the last of the world's great empires, for with its fate is sealed the fate of all the nations. " '. . . Babylon is fallen, fallen, that great city, because she made all nations drink of the wine of the wrath of her fornication' " (Rev. 14:8).

> "And the kings of the earth who have committed fornication and lived luxuriously with her will weep and lament for her, when they see the smoke of her burning, standing at a distance for fear of her torment, saying, 'Alas, alas, that great city Babylon, that mighty city! For in one hour your judgment has come.' And the merchants of the earth will weep and mourn over her, for no one buys their merchandise anymore.
>
> ". . . And every shipmaster, all who travel by ship, sailors, and as many as trade on the sea, stood at a distance and cried out when they saw the smoke of her burning, saying 'What is like this great city! . . . For in one hour she is made desolate' " (Rev. 18:9–11, 17–19).

In one hour all the glory and luxury of the world will fall apart. It had gone whoring with Islam and let itself be bound to the oil countries. The whole "economic miracle" will tumble like a house of cards.

> " 'Alas! for that day is great, there is none like it; and it is the time of Jacob's distress . . .' " (Jer. 30:7).

> . . . The day of the LORD is indeed great and very awesome, and who can endure it (Joel 2:11)?

> Lift up a signal in the land, blow a trumpet among the nations! Consecrate the nations against her, summon against her the kingdoms of Ararat, Minni and Ashkenaz; appoint a marshal against her, bring up the horses like bristly locusts (Jer. 51:27).

> "And it will come about in that day that I will set about to destroy all the nations that come against Jerusalem" (Zech. 12:9).

Thus, the last world empire and the nations supported by it, as well as the colossus that stood on Babylon's soil (not Italy's), will be destroyed by the Lord from heaven.

> "And I will pour out on the house of David and on the inhabitants of Jerusalem, the Spirit of grace and of supplication, so that they will look on Me whom they have pierced; and they will mourn for Him . . ." (Zech. 12:10).

9

Watch and Be Ready

Repeatedly Jesus told His followers to watch for His return. As recorded by Luke, He said: " 'Nation will rise against nation. . . . And there will be great earthquakes in various places, and famines and pestilences. . . . And you will be hated by all for My name's sake. . . . And when you see Jerusalem surrounded by armies, then know that its desolation is near. . . . Now when these things begin to happen, look up and lift up your heads, because your redemption draws near' " (Luke 21:10,11,17,20,28).

These things that Jesus mentioned and others that we have seen throughout the Scriptures have begun to happen. The coming weeks and years are going to be difficult ones, particularly for those in the West. For those with nothing to depend on, despair will set in. Skeptics will say, ". . . 'Where is the promise of His coming? For since the fathers fell asleep, all things continue as they were from the beginning of creation' " (2 Pet. 3:4). Yet their skepticism does not alter the fact that the Lord will return.

In the immediate future we will become more and more dependent on the Arabs. We have no chance of survival if the Arabs shut off the oil flow. And that is just what they have threatened to do. But the greater danger to us is not a shortage of oil, but Islam itself. The Arabs believe they have received their oil from Allah, and they will use it as an instrument for the attainment of world domination for Allah. They will let nothing stand in their way.

The Russians are playing a more and more important role in the Middle East, and their support is clearly for the Arabs. After the assassination of King Faisal and the obvious failure of Kissinger's policies, things changed in favor of the Soviet Union within a week. Whether there will be another war in the Middle East or a temporary negotiated peace, the Soviets will play a key role. They will be weapons-deliverers, mediators, or both.

A few days before the murder of Faisal, a Russian said: "The risk of war in the Middle East is greater than ever. We know that neither the United States nor we ourselves can control our warring allies entirely." The PLO leader, Yasir Arafat, believes a war is imminent, and Zouheir Mohsen, a former leader of the military division of the PLO, says a fifth Middle East war is coming. He emphasized in an interview for the Lebanese magazine *As Sayyad* that the outbreak of this war depends totally on Israel's behavior. According to Mohsen, the United States has supplied Israel with enough weapons to last through twenty-five days of uninterrupted fighting, and as long as Israel continues to arm and elevate itself above the Arab world, there will be no peace in the Middle East. (Mohsen has been assassinated since this interview.) He felt the Soviet Union would withdraw its recognition of Israel and would demand the exclusion of Israel from the UN. In

Territories of Islamic Majority

Nearly 800 million Muslims—a fifth of the world's population.

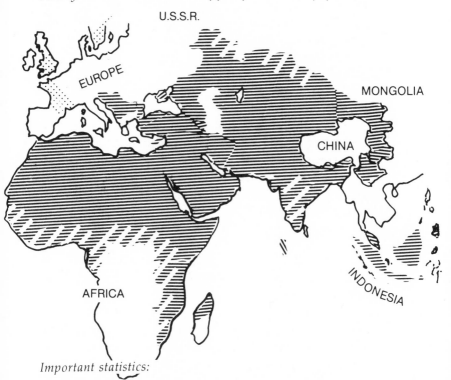

Important statistics:

USSR—50 million Muslims, 15.5% of the population;
China—17 million Muslims, 2% of the population.

May, 1974, Andrei Gromyko, the Soviet Foreign Minister, said in a visit to Damascus: "I do not need to reassure you that the Soviet Union stands firmly for the termination of Israeli occupation of all annexed territories. All other questions are unimportant when compared with this one."

195

The Soviet Union's role as a supplier of weapons to the Arab world is well documented. According to United Press International specialist Carol Tailor, the Russians recently delivered one hundred and fifty ground missiles to the Syrians, all of which can reach the cities of Israel. This shipment enormously strengthened Syria's military potential. Further deliveries should bring the number to two hundred. Expert opinion sees an enormous armament competition going on in the Middle East in which the quantity and quality of military goods on both sides are growing alarmingly. When we see the armament race in the Middle East, we must ask ourselves how far we are from the battle of Armageddon.

Atomic Weapons

Most of the arms build-up in the Middle East is occurring with conventional weapons and being done under the pretext of maintaining a balance of power to guarantee peace. However, a more desperate situation could quickly develop with the threatened use of atomic weapons. Fortunately such a specter is still on the horizon, but just a short distance away. In 1966 Nasser threatened to start a program of nuclear weapons development if Israel did not officially declare that it neither possessed nor was in the process of developing nuclear armaments. Fortunately the Soviet Union did not support him at the time, saying only that Egypt could be assured of Russian protection if Israel should produce atomic weapons. Presumably this guarantee is still valid.

The question of the development of atomic energy

by Arab states was first brought up at a summit conference in Algiers in November, 1973. It gave new impetus to the General Arabic Scientific Council.

> In May, 1974, the military department of the Arab League demanded the equipping of the Arab armies with atomic weapons. The Arab kings want to hire foreign scientists to develop an atomic bomb in Saudi Arabia.[1]

In spite of the potential threat of atomic weapons, neither side in the Middle East conflict has become more cautious. Conventional conflicts occur with a distressing degree of regularity, because so far both sides possess significant arsenals and do not need to use atomic weapons.

However, a renewed round of military activity seems inevitable, and there is the threat of Tel Aviv's using non-conventional weapons. So far Israel has survived its battles with the Arabs by using its blitzkrieg attacks. But the Arabs' economic and military potential is said to be such that today Israel has no chance of surviving a drawn-out engagement *unless it uses atomic weapons.* Since the Arabs may also have such arms at their disposal, the Israelis may be forced to strike with a nuclear attack first.

It won't be long before the Arabs realize that their weapon of oil is stronger than any bomb—atomic or otherwise. They will eventually try to destroy Israel by placing a complete oil embargo on any land not willing to take the Arab position against Israel. The Arabs will become more and more set against any attempt at peace.

No matter what shape the next conflict takes, the result will be favorable to the fourth beast, the Muslim bloc led by Iraq. Revelation 13:2 will become a reality: ". . . And the dragon gave him his power, his throne, and great authority." This "great authority" means control over sources of energy and money. The world will be forced again in a pointed way with the choice of worshiping God or mammon.

Iron and Clay

The Arab world is like a fortress that Mohammed surrounded with a high fence: Islam and its culture. For more than a thousand years followers of Mohammed were isolated from the rest of the world. Western explorers died searching out Africa and the Middle East, yet even today it is impossible for a non-Muslim to visit the holy city of Mecca. The Islamic culture has for so long been inaccessible and isolated that today it is impossible for it to assimilate foreign elements. The West has different traditions, a different culture, and a different religion. The two worlds are in conflict, and even if they wanted to could not be combined.

This is why the alliance between Russia and the Arabic countries is so difficult: Russia is essentially Western in outlook; the Arabic countries of the Middle East are Islamic. Yet Russia is preparing the way for the fourth beast. It is like a red carpet for Islam. No country of Europe or Asia must deal with Islam as carefully as the Soviet Union because about fifty million Muslims live within its borders, and the number is growing rapidly. Those in Caucasus and Central Asia form a society of their own and, like their counterparts in the Arabic countries, they are awakening from a long sleep. This is worrisome to the Soviets; they do not want to underestimate or oppress such a large minority.

In Daniel 2, the prophet told Nebuchadnezzar of one of the king's past dreams that had been forgotten. In the dream Nebuchadnezzar had seen a giant statue made out of four metals: The head was fine gold, the breast and arms were silver, the belly and thighs were brass, and the legs were iron. The feet, however, were iron mixed with clay. The four basic sections of the statue refer to the same four kingdoms as the four beasts in the vision recorded in Daniel 7. Daniel explained the feet:

> "And as the toes of the feet were partly of iron and partly of pottery, so some of the kingdom will be strong and part of it will be brittle" (Dan. 2:43).

Men are striving to break down the barriers between the West and Islam, but it will not work. In the alliance between the Arabs and the Russians we can see the feet of the giant statue. Iron and clay do not mix, and neither will the West and Islam.

Since the events in Iran, Saudi Arabia has changed its course. Other than Iran, it had been the only pro-West, pro-American land in the Middle East. It had rejected the Soviet Union as being an atheistic land, but now it is flirting with the Russian atheists. On April 1, 1979, the Saudis resolved to limit their oil production to 8.5 million barrels per day, although the world needs 16 million barrels. Causes of this reduction were stated to be America's Middle East policy and Egypt's peace treaty with Israel. How long will the West be able to live with this situation?

Any alliance of Saudis and Russians is of course doomed to failure from the very beginning, for clay and iron do not mix. This alliance, if it takes place, will be destroyed by the Stone from heaven, unaided by human hands.

The Dragon Laughs

The dizzying arms build-up in the Middle East by both the Soviet Union and the United States is well known, and this powder keg could explode much more easily than is commonly believed. Only the fuse is necessary, some small incident that could set off a full-scale conflict. The world is preparing its own destruction and will hold God responsible!

The dragon is laughing, for the world is intently working to reach his goals: the spiritual and then the material annihilation of mankind. This catastrophe will break upon our world in a flash. Three times in Revelation (18:10,17,19) John emphasized that the glory of the city of Babylon will be destroyed in one hour, causing the world's economy to grind to a halt. Given today's conditions, it is not difficult to imagine such a thing happening.

When the fuse is lit, Russia, America, and Europe will all be drawn into the conflict because they are so deeply involved in the Middle East. We have seen something of Russia's involvement, but America is committed to helping the Arabs as well. It is interesting that America supports both sides in the conflict,

Arabs as well as Israelis. In September, 1979, the Associated Press reported:

> America wants to build the Saudis a new defense ministry modeled on their own Pentagon. According to official Washington sources, the complex will be equipped with an underground commando outpost, a mosque, a cafeteria, and parking areas. The Saudis are prepared to spend 500 million dollars for it. America will handle the construction of accessory streets and the landscaping.

Preparations are being made and lines are being drawn for Armaggedon. Previous battles will seem to be nothing compared to the final battle of the superpowers in the Middle East.

> "And you will come from your place out of the remote parts of the north, you and many peoples with you, all of them riding on horses, a great assembly and a mighty army; and you will come up against My people Israel like a cloud to cover the land. It will come about in the last days that I shall bring you against My land, in order that the nations may know Me when I shall be sanctified through you before their eyes, O Gog" (Ezek. 38:15,16).

> "And it will come about in that day that I will set about to destroy all the nations that come against Jerusalem" (Zech. 12:9).

> Then the Lord will go forth and fight against those nations, as when He fights on a day of battle (Zech. 14:3).

> And I saw the beast, the kings of the earth, and their armies, gathered together to make war against Him who sat on the horse and against His army (Rev. 19:19).

As the Bible clearly states, Israel has become a burden for many nations. We already know the outcome of this "battle against God and His Anointed." The kings of the earth from the east to west will unite on the side of the Beast and march against Israel, not realizing that they are fighting against God and His son Jesus Christ. All the war apparatus of the nations is stamped with the words "in vain," for no matter how much the world tries, it cannot escape God and His Anointed One.

Mankind has learned nothing from its past mistakes. In wanting to be rid of the "problems" of Israel and of God, it is only serving the interests of the evil one. Both Israel and the rest of the nations will recognize the One whom they have pierced only when they have gone through apocalyptic fires.

Jerusalem: Tragedy on Center Stage

> Blow a trumpet in Zion, and sound an alarm on My holy mountain! Let all the inhabitants of the land tremble, for the day of the Lord is coming; surely it is near. A day of darkness and gloom, a day of clouds and thick darkness . . . (Joel 2:1).

God's holy mountain is in Jerusalem, the city He has chosen as His holy city (see Zech. 1:17). But Satan has chosen this city too, and there will be no rest in the Islamic world as long as Jerusalem remains in Jewish control. On November 9, 1978, Yasir Arafat summoned all Muslims to a holy war against Israel to liberate the city and especially the Al Aqsa mosque. In August, 1980, Saudi Arabia's Crown Prince Fahd also called for a *jihad* for the liberation of Jerusalem.

For the nations of the world, the coming battle will be a moment of truth. But God will make a glorious day out of the chaos, because Jesus Christ will intervene to shorten the battle and usher in a new age, the millennial kingdom of peace.

The more intensely the nations seek a compromise solution, the deeper they will sink into a quagmire of chaos and the faster they will bring on their own destruction. The world rejoiced at the Israeli-Egyptian peace treaty hammered out at Camp David. But the treaty cannot possibly last since God Himself will reject it. It is not His peace plan.

Man cannot transgress God's laws and remain unscathed. God will not save mankind from the coming chaos because that would be negating His own decrees. He has given men once and for all the opportunity to escape the coming wrath through His crucified Son. There is no escape for those who do not accept this offer; they can only await judgment.

Of course, the Camp David accords were not warmly received by the Arab nations, other than Egypt, because they did not really solve the Jerusalem problem. To the Arab mind the only solution is akin to the Bible's picture of a strong man taking over the city in the end times and the armies of the Beast and the

False Prophet calling for the annihilation of the Jewish people.

Today there is a gathering of religious and military forces such as the world has never seen. The armies of the earth will march on Mount Moriah, and the arsenal around Armageddon will be stocked with the newest, most modern weapons. The eyes of the Beast will be on the temple in Jerusalem. Faisal has said, "If we threaten the world, it is only to liberate Jerusalem." God has said,

> "Behold, I am going to make Jerusalem a cup that causes reeling to all the peoples around; and when the seige is against Jerusalem, it will also be against Judah. And it will come about in that day that I will make Jerusalem a heavy stone for all the peoples; all who lift it will be severely injured. And all the nations of the earth will be gathered against it" (Zech. 12:2,3).

> For I will gather all the nations against Jerusalem to battle, and the city will be captured, the houses plundered, the women ravished, and half of the city exiled, but the rest of the people will not be cut off from the city (Zech. 14:2).

Peace will only come when Israel and the nations of the world acknowledge that "no other foundation can anyone lay than that which is laid, which is Jesus Christ" (1 Cor. 3:11).

10

The End

Throughout history mankind has searched for a new society, one in which there will be peace, equality, and material well-being. The United Nations was formed with the vision of bringing a lasting peace to the world. But although the UN can claim some success, the world is no more peaceful today than it was in 1945 when the organization was founded.

Equality is an ideal that most people defend. And yet what is really meant is that equality is desired for one's self, not necessarily for the other person. An example of this was described earlier. Muslims want—and are granted—equality in the Western world to build mosques and win converts for Islam, but Christians are denied the right to preach the gospel in Islamic countries. Material well-being is an elusive goal, for people always want more. And in fact, the distribution of material goods in the world is becoming less balanced as the Arabs amass vast amounts of wealth so quickly that they hardly know what to do with it all.

But mankind is always hopeful that a new society will come. We know that we live in a world of war, but we hope for peace. We know that man is selfish, but we dream of a world in which all are treated as equals. We know that exploitation is occurring so that some people have little hope of material well-being, yet we proclaim that all people should have the basic material needs of life. The new society that mankind dreams of and politicians promise will remain utopian as long as individuals are not born again by the Spirit of God. Without Christ, society cannot better itself and is actually heading in the other direction.

The Failure of the New Society

For several hundred years the West has been trying to create a new society, but it is losing the ability to continue. The West will realize what power it possessed only when that power has been totally taken away. Because of the West's unfaithfulness, it is too late. The future of the West is not one of peace, equality, and material well-being, but one of war, hatred, and bankruptcy.

Three hundred years ago the forces of Islam stood at the door of the West, about to tear it down. Islam was successfully rebuffed. Today the forces of Islam are preparing to invade the West in a more subtle, yet successful way.

Although economic, military, and political factors will weigh heavily in the coming battle, it will essentially be one of a spiritual nature. The forces of darkness can only be held in check through God's Spirit. But after the Rapture of the church, described in 1 Thessalonians 4:13–18, the spirit of the Antichrist and the False Prophet will have free reign. The chaos will be complete.

The purpose of this book has been to show those who rejoice in the hope of the appearing of the Son of God just how near we are to His coming. Christians can lift up their eyes because they know that their salvation is approaching. The church will not experience the final phase of the anti-Christian reign on earth. It should have become clear to many reading this book just how serious the current situation is and that any hope outside of Christ is no hope at all.

But the West is continuing to try to build a new society by itself—without God. Martin Luther's majestic hymn "A Mighty Fortress Is Our God" says,

> Did we in our own strength confide,
> Our striving would be losing,
> Were not the right Man on our side,
> The Man of God's own choosing.
>
> Dost ask who that may be?
> Christ Jesus, it is He!
> Lord Sabaoth His name,
> From age to age the same,
> And He must win the battle.

The West has put its confidence in its own strength. It has excluded "the Man of God's own choosing," Jesus Christ, from its thinking. He has been forced out of our families, where we no longer pray with our children and study the Word of God together, just as He has been shut out of the government. Compare the prevailing attitude in the West with that in Saudi Arabia where prayer is sacred. Five times a day stores close, politicians stop their work, all activities come to a standstill as everyone says his prayers.

The West is trying to build a new society without God. But the word that will be final is found in 1 Corinthians 1:19,20. Paul asks,

> For it is written: "I will destroy the wisdom of the wise, and bring to nothing the understanding of the prudent." Where is the wise? Where is the scribe? Where is the disputer of this age? Has not God made foolish the wisdom of this world?

The answer is given in the next verse: "For since, in the wisdom of God, the world by wisdom did not know God, it pleased God by the foolishness of the message preached to save those who believe."

The Hope of a New Life

The battle against God and His anointed One is rapidly coming to a head. Only the Holy Spirit is preventing warfare from erupting on a grand scale, and He will be removed at the Rapture of the church. Mankind's efforts at building a new society by himself are failing, but the believer in Jesus puts his hope in a new life. The Christian can look to the future with confidence and joy, knowing that he will forever be with the Lord Jesus in the presence of the Father. Even in the middle of a troubled world, he knows that Christ said:

> "Peace I leave with you, My peace I give to you; not as the world gives do I give to you. Let not your heart be troubled, neither let it be afraid. You have heard how I said to you, 'I am going away and coming back to you.' If you loved Me,

you would rejoice because I said, 'I am going to the Father,' for My Father is greater than I. And now I have told you before it comes to pass, that when it comes to pass, you may believe" (John 14:27–29).

The nations of the world have created a maze for themselves and now are seeking a way out. But the harder they search, the more confused they become. Jesus Christ is the Way, the only Truth, and the Life. The answer to the troubled future of the world is not to be found in a new society, but in a new life.

Therefore, if anyone is in Christ, he is a new creation; old things have passed away; behold, all things have become new (2 Cor. 5:17).

In spite of the disastrous predictions we see for the future of the world, we still live today in an age of grace. The door to Christ's kingdom remains open to all: to Jews, to heathen, and to Muslims. There is no difference; God does not treat people differently. His offer of new life is the same to all. He will make you a new person and give you a hope in spite of coming world events if you will only put your trust in Jesus Christ.

For God so loved the world that He gave His only begotten Son, that whoever believes in Him should not perish but have everlasting life (John 3:16).

You cannot trust your own abilities, the promises of politicians, or another god for your future well-being.

You can trust only Jesus Christ. He does not make a false promise of a new society here on earth, but he will give you a new life to withstand the turmoil around you.

This age is quickly coming to a close. It is the most interesting time since the birth of the church nearly two thousand years ago. The prophets and apostles wished to see what we are seeing today. Therefore we should prepare ourselves for Christ's coming and redeem the time so that we can go to meet Him joyfully. Jesus will unite the members of His body to Himself, the Head, so that He may present them to the Father "a glorious church, not having spot or wrinkle . . . holy and without blemish" (Eph. 5:27). If we belong to this body, our prayer and our longing will be for Christ's return.

> And the Spirit and the bride say, "Come!" And let him who hears say, "Come!" And let him who thirst come. And whoever desires, let him take the water of life freely (Rev. 22:17).

We must realize that Israel has a mission in the end times. Its formation as a nation in 1948 and the declaration of Jerusalem as its capital in 1980 are important steps in preparing it for that mission. We must realize that the age of the Gentiles has ended. We must also realize that the church of Jesus Christ is not primarily an earthly institution, and its purpose is not political. In view of the current end times, we must take seriously the words of the apostle Paul.

> "There is none who understands; there is none who seeks after God. They have all gone out of

210

the way; they have together become unprofit-
able; there is none who does good, no, not one.
Their throat is an open tomb; with their tongues
they have practiced deceit, the poison of asps is
under their lips, whose mouth is full of cursing
and bitterness" (Rom. 3:11–14).

If we walk closely with the Lord, we will be able to
say to Him when we see Him face to face,

I have fought the good fight, I have finished the
race, I have kept the faith. Finally, there is laid up
for me the crown of righteousness, which the
Lord, the righteous Judge, will give me on that
Day; and not to me only, but also to all who have
loved His appearing (2 Tim. 4:7,8).

In the great Tribulation there will still be those who
believe and follow God. They will not be members of
the church, which will be gone, but they will be
followers of Jesus Christ.

Only after the great Tribulation will the longed-for
kingdom of peace come—a true new society—in
which justice will prevail. Justice, faith, peace, and the
eternal Word of God will go forth from the new
Jerusalem, the city held in such high esteem by all the
monotheistic religions of the world. The Lord will be
the judge over the earth and will punish all the nations. Only then will the quote from Isaiah found near
the UN building become a reality:

. . . And they will hammer their swords into
plowshares, and their spears into pruning
hooks. Nation will not lift up sword against
nation, and never again will they learn war (Is.
2:4).

Notes

Chapter 1

1. Abdullah, *Jesus: Life, Commission, Death* (Hamburg-Stellingen: Ahmadiyya Islam Mission, 1960), p. 4.
2. *Historie de l'Empire Othoman* (1713).
3. *Welt am Sonntag*, Sept. 3, 1978.
4. *Les Dernières Nouvelles d'Alsace*, Sept. 5, 1978.
5. Anton Zischka, Europe's Threatened Main Artery (Berne: Kümmerly & Frey, 1976), p. 118.
6. Ray Vicker, "Arabs Buying up U.S.?" *Wall Street Journal*, July 18, 1980.
7. "Les Arabes," *Encyclopédie du Monde Actuel* (1975) p.54.
8. J. P. Roux, *L'Aslam au Proche Orient* (Paris: Payot, 1960), pp. 19–20.
9. Gerhard Konzelmann, *Rich Men of the East* (Munich: Verlag Kurt, 1975), p. 11.
10. Ibid.

Chapter 2

1. Jens Friedemann, *The Sheiks Are Coming* (Bergish Gladbach: Lubbe, 1974), p. 46.
2. Gerhard Konzelmann, *The Arabs* (Munich: F. A. Herbig Verlagsbuchhandlung, 1974), pp. 11–12.
3. *Aachener Nachrichten*, Feb. 17, 1976.

4. *Dernières Nouvelles*, April 13, 1976.
5. Ibid., April 9, 1976.
6. Bureau of Economic Analysis, U.S. Department of Commerce, June, 1980.
7. *Dernières Nouvelles*, Jan. 31, 1978.
8. *Dernières Nouvelles d'Alsace*, Aug. 2, 1978.
9. *Nouvel Observateur*, May 22, 1978.
10. Vicker, "Arabs Buying up U.S.?"
11. *Dernières Nouvelles d'Alsace*, Oct. 30, 1975.
12. Friedemann, *The Sheiks Are Coming*.
13. *Express*, Numero Spécial, Dec. 1974.

Chapter 3

1. Zischka, *Europe's Threatened Main Artery*.
2. Seymour Kurtz, ed., *The New York Times Encyclopedic Almanac*: 1970 (New York: *New York Times*, 1979), p. 436.
3. Will Durant, *The Age of Faith*, Vol. 4 (New York: Simon & Schuster, 1954).
4. Konrad Meyer, "The Middle East at the Crossroads," (September, 1975), p. 11.
5. John Alden Williams, ed., *Islam* (New York: George Braziller, 1962), pp. 31-32.
6. Richard Muller, *Thou Who Art in Heaven* (n.p.).
7. These thoughts are chosen from Henry M. Morris, *Bible and Modern Science* (Chicago: Moody Press, 1956).
8. Robert H. Glover, *The Progress of World-Wide Missions*, rev. by. J. Herbert Kane (New York: Harper & Row, 1960), p. 30.
9. Konzelmann, *Rich Men of the East*.
10. Mirella Bianco, *Qaddafi, Messenger from the Desert* (Paris: Editions Stock, 1974), pp. 183, 187.
11. Zischka, *Europe's Threatened Main Artery*.

NOTES

Chapter 4.

1. Claude Duvernoy, *The Zionism of God* (Paris: Serg, 1970), p. 276.
2. *Bruckenbauer*, Biel.
3. P. Henri Nusslé, "Dialogue with Islam, *Edition de l'Action Chrétienne en Orient*, Dec. 8, 1949, p. 50.
4. Ibid.
5. Wolfgang G. Lerch, *Frankfurter Allgemeine*, Sept. 9, 1978.
6. *Neue Weltschau*, Dec. 12, 1974.
7. Marcel Schwander, in a Swiss newspaper, 1978.
8. Martina Kempff, *Die Welt*, Apr. 17, 1979.
9. Konzelmann, *The Arabs*.
10. Maurice Bucaille, *The Bible, The Qur'an & Science* (Indianapolis: American Trust Publications, 1978).
11. *Hebdo*, Feb. 13-19, 1976.
12. *Christ in der Gegenwart*, Apr. 23, 1978 (Freiburg in Breisgau: Verlag Herder).

Chapter 5

2. Martin Luther, *Jesus Christ, a Born Jew* (n.p.).
2. Ibid.
3. Friedrich Heer, *God's First Love* (Munich: Verlag Bechtle, 1967), p. 67.
4. Ibid.
5. Duvernoy, *The Zionism of God*.
6. E. Guers, *The Destiny of Israel* (1964).
7. Dr. Griffin in ibid.
8. *Weltwoche*, Feb. 7, 1979.
9. Erich Sauer, *Dawn of the World Redemption* (Grand Rapids: Eerdmans, 1951).

Chapter 6

1. "The Muslims, Our Neighbors" (German Protestant Council on Missions).

215

2. Zischka, *Europe's Threatened Main Artery*.
3. "Three Thousand Princes Dream of Entering Jerusalem," *Die Welt*, June, 1979.

Chapter 7

1. Gerhard Bergman, *Uproar About the Bible* (Aussaat: Wuppertal, 1974), p. 14.
2. Heinz Zahrnt, *Allgemeinen Deutschen Sonntagsblatt* (1960).
3. Abdullah, *Jesus—Life, Mission, and Death*.
4. Ibid.
5. Ibid.
6. Ibid.
7. Ibid.
8. Ibid.
9. Ibid.
10. Abdul Hatif, head of the Ahmadiyya in Germany.

Chapter 8.

1. José Fralon, *Europe Is Finished* (Paris: Calmann-Lévy).
2. *Stern*, May 10, 1979.
3. *Neues Bülacher Tagblatt*, July 1, 1974.
4. H. G. Behr, *Sons of the Desert* (Düsseldorf: Econ, n.d.), p. 342.

Chapter 9

1. Konzelmann, *Rich Men of the East*.